# TEACHER GUIDE

**4th–6th Grade**

Includes Worksheets

Apologetics

Weekly Lesson Schedule

Answer Key

# Elementary Apologetics

First printing: January 2017
Fourth printing: May 2018

Copyright © 2017 by Master Books®. All rights reserved. No part of this book may be used or reproduced in any manner whatsoever without written permission of the publisher, except in the case of brief quotations in articles and reviews.
For information write:

Master Books®, P.O. Box 726, Green Forest, AR 72638

Master Books® is a division of the New Leaf Publishing Group, Inc.

ISBN: 978-1-68344-026-0
ISBN: 978-1-61458-582-4 (digital)

Unless otherwise noted, Scripture quotations are from the New King James Version of the Bible.

**Printed in the United States of America**

Please visit our website for other great titles:
www.masterbooks.com

For information regarding author interviews,
please contact the publicity department at (870) 438-5288.

Permission is granted for copies of reproducible pages from this text to be made for use within your own homeschooling family activities. Material may not be posted online, distributed digitally, or made available as a download. Permission for any other use of the material must be requested prior to use by email to the publisher at info@nlpg.com.

> Your reputation as a publisher is stellar. It is a blessing knowing anything I purchase from you is going to be worth every penny!
> —Cheri ★★★★★

> Last year we found Master Books and it has made a HUGE difference.
> —Melanie ★★★★★

> We love Master Books and the way it's set up for easy planning!
> —Melissa ★★★★★

> You have done a great job. MASTER BOOKS ROCKS!
> —Stephanie ★★★★★

> Physically high-quality, Biblically faithful, and well-written.
> —Danika ★★★★★

> Best books ever. Their illustrations are captivating and content amazing!
> —Kathy ★★★★★

**Affordable**
**Flexible**
**Faith Building**

# Table of Contents

Using This Teacher Guide ................................................................................................ 4
Course Objectives ............................................................................................................ 4
Course Description .......................................................................................................... 5
Suggested Daily Schedule ................................................................................................ 7
Worksheets ..................................................................................................................... 15
Quizzes ......................................................................................................................... 171
Answers for Worksheets and Quizzes ........................................................................... 185

# Using This Teacher Guide

**Features:** The suggested weekly schedule enclosed has easy-to-manage lessons that guide the reading, worksheets, and all assessments. The pages of this guide are perforated and three-hole punched so materials are easy to tear out, hand out, grade, and store. Teachers are encouraged to adjust the schedule and materials needed in order to best work within their unique educational program.

**Lesson Scheduling:** Students are instructed to read the pages in their book and then complete the corresponding section provided by the teacher. Assessments that may include worksheets, activities, quizzes, and tests are given at regular intervals with space to record each grade. Space is provided on the weekly schedule for assignment dates, and flexibility in scheduling is encouraged. Teachers may adapt the scheduled days per each unique student situation. As the student completes each assignment, this can be marked with an "X" in the box.

| | |
|---|---|
| 🕐 | Approximately 30 to 45 minutes per lesson, four days a week |
| 🔑 | Includes answer keys for worksheets and quizzes |
| 📝 | Worksheets for each lesson |
| 📄 | Quizzes are included to help reinforce learning and provide assessment opportunities |
| 🔄 | Designed for grades 4 to 6 in a one-year course |

**Course Objectives:** Students completing this course will

- Investigate biblical truths concerning the creation account, Adam and Eve, and sin
- Become familiar with God's Word, what He desires of them, and how much He loves them
- Identify insights regarding the account of Noah and the Ark, how he and his family cared for the animals, and how fossils formed
- Learn how to defend their faith against a secular worldview in a fallen world
- Study truths about the Tower of Babel, the Ice Age, and the purpose of stars
- Write out text they can share with friends or family about what they have learned

# Course Description

Based on the amazing *Answers Books for Kids* series, with answers to over 100 of their most difficult questions! This course features a four-day schedule, Monday through Thursday, but is easily adaptable to most any educational calendar.

This apologetics study for upper elementary children delves into issues regarding the Bible, God, sin, dinosaurs, the Flood of Noah, salvation, astronomy, and more, and is all based on actual questions asked by kids. Answers are important. If children aren't given answers to their questions about the Bible and the history it reveals, they cannot defend their faith against a fallen world. The course highlights the unique collection of question-answer books from Ken Ham and the creative team at Answers in Genesis to meet this need and helps kids focus on Scripture memorization and faith-building truth. The Bible verses quoted in *The Answers Book for Kids* series are from the New King James Version, though kids are encouraged to write out their daily verses in the version they use each day. Note: Some memory verses and verses to write out are repeated.

**Quizzes:** Quizzes are optional and should be assigned at the teacher's discretion. The maturity of the student should determine whether the quizzes are open book.

**Grading Options for This Course:** It is always the prerogative of an educator to assess student grades however he or she might deem best. The following is only a suggested guideline based on the material presented through this course:

To calculate the percentage of the worksheets and quizzes, the educator may use the following guide. Divide total number of questions correct (example: 43) by the total number of questions possible (example: 46) to calculate the percentage out of 100 possible. 43/46 = 93 percent correct.

The suggested grade values are noted as follows: 90 to 100 percent = A; 80 to 89 percent = B; 70 to 79 percent = C; 60 to 69 percent = D; and 0 to 59 percent = F.

# First Semester Suggested Daily Schedule

| Date | Day | Assignment | Due Date | ✓ | Grade |
|---|---|---|---|---|---|
| | | First Semester-First Quarter | | | |
| Week 1 | Day 1 | Read pages 4–5 (*The Answers Book for Kids Volume 1*)<br>Complete Worksheet 1 (*Teacher Guide*, page 17) | | | |
| | Day 2 | Read pages 6–7 (*The Answers Book for Kids Volume 1*)<br>Complete Worksheet 2 (*Teacher Guide*, page 18) | | | |
| | Day 3 | Read pages 8–9 (*The Answers Book for Kids Volume 1*)<br>Complete Worksheet 3 (*Teacher Guide*, page 19) | | | |
| | Day 4 | Read pages 10–11 (*The Answers Book for Kids Volume 1*)<br>Complete Worksheet 4 (*Teacher Guide*, page 20) | | | |
| | Day 5 | Free day/study day | | | |
| Week 2 | Day 6 | Read pages 12–13 (*The Answers Book for Kids Volume 1*)<br>Complete Worksheet 5 (*Teacher Guide*, page 21) | | | |
| | Day 7 | Read pages 14–15 (*The Answers Book for Kids Volume 1*)<br>Complete Worksheet 6 (*Teacher Guide*, page 22) | | | |
| | Day 8 | Read pages 16–17 (*The Answers Book for Kids Volume 1*)<br>Complete Worksheet 7 (*Teacher Guide*, page 23) | | | |
| | Day 9 | Read pages 18–19 (*The Answers Book for Kids Volume 1*)<br>Complete Worksheet 8 (*Teacher Guide*, page 24) | | | |
| | Day 10 | Free day/study day | | | |
| Week 3 | Day 11 | Read pages 20–21 (*The Answers Book for Kids Volume 1*)<br>Complete Worksheet 9 (*Teacher Guide*, page 25) | | | |
| | Day 12 | Read pages 22–23 (*The Answers Book for Kids Volume 1*)<br>Complete Worksheet 10 (*Teacher Guide*, page 26) | | | |
| | Day 13 | Read pages 24–25 (*The Answers Book for Kids Volume 1*)<br>Complete Worksheet 11 (*Teacher Guide*, page 27) | | | |
| | Day 14 | Read pages 26–27 (*The Answers Book for Kids Volume 1*)<br>Complete Worksheet 12 (*Teacher Guide*, page 28) | | | |
| | Day 15 | Free day/study day | | | |
| Week 4 | Day 16 | Read pages 28–29 (*The Answers Book for Kids Volume 1*)<br>Complete Worksheet 13 (*Teacher Guide*, page 29) | | | |
| | Day 17 | Read pages 30–31 (*The Answers Book for Kids Volume 1*)<br>Complete Worksheet 14 (*Teacher Guide*, page 30) | | | |
| | Day 18 | Read pages 32–33 (*The Answers Book for Kids Volume 1*)<br>Complete Worksheet 15 (*Teacher Guide*, page 31) | | | |
| | Day 19 | Read pages 34–35 (*The Answers Book for Kids Volume 1*)<br>Complete Worksheet 16 (*Teacher Guide*, page 32) | | | |
| | Day 20 | Free day/study day | | | |
| Week 5 | Day 21 | Read pages 36–37 (*The Answers Book for Kids Volume 1*)<br>Complete Worksheet 17 (*Teacher Guide*, page 33) | | | |
| | Day 22 | Read pages 38–39 (*The Answers Book for Kids Volume 1*)<br>Complete Worksheet 18 (*Teacher Guide*, page 34) | | | |
| | Day 23 | Read pages 40–41 (*The Answers Book for Kids Volume 1*)<br>Complete Worksheet 19 (*Teacher Guide*, page 35) | | | |
| | Day 24 | Read pages 42–43 (*The Answers Book for Kids Volume 1*)<br>Complete Worksheet 20 (*Teacher Guide*, page 36) | | | |
| | Day 25 | Free day/study day | | | |

| Date | Day | Assignment | Due Date | ✓ | Grade |
|---|---|---|---|---|---|
| Week 6 | Day 26 | Read pages 44–45 (*The Answers Book for Kids Volume 1*)<br>Complete Worksheet 21 (*Teacher Guide*, page 37) | | | |
| | Day 27 | Read pages 46–47 (*The Answers Book for Kids Volume 1*)<br>Complete Worksheet 22 (*Teacher Guide*, page 38) | | | |
| | Day 28 | Quiz 1 (*Teacher Guide*, page 173) | | | |
| | Day 29 | Complete Worksheet 23 (*Teacher Guide*, page 39) | | | |
| | Day 30 | Free day/study day | | | |
| Week 7 | Day 31 | Read pages 4–5 (*The Answers Book for Kids Volume 2*)<br>Complete Worksheet 24 (*Teacher Guide*, page 43) | | | |
| | Day 32 | Read pages 6–7 (*The Answers Book for Kids Volume 2*)<br>Complete Worksheet 25 (*Teacher Guide*, page 44) | | | |
| | Day 33 | Read pages 8–9 (*The Answers Book for Kids Volume 2*)<br>Complete Worksheet 26 (*Teacher Guide*, page 45) | | | |
| | Day 34 | Read pages 10–11 (*The Answers Book for Kids Volume 2*)<br>Complete Worksheet 27 (*Teacher Guide*, page 46) | | | |
| | Day 35 | Free day/study day | | | |
| Week 8 | Day 36 | Read pages 12–13 (*The Answers Book for Kids Volume 2*)<br>Complete Worksheet 28 (*Teacher Guide*, page 47) | | | |
| | Day 37 | Read pages 14–15 (*The Answers Book for Kids Volume 2*)<br>Complete Worksheet 29 (*Teacher Guide*, page 48) | | | |
| | Day 38 | Read pages 16–17 (*The Answers Book for Kids Volume 2*)<br>Complete Worksheet 30 (*Teacher Guide*, page 49) | | | |
| | Day 39 | Read pages 18–19 (*The Answers Book for Kids Volume 2*)<br>Complete Worksheet 31 (*Teacher Guide*, page 50) | | | |
| | Day 40 | Free day/study day | | | |
| Week 9 | Day 41 | Read pages 20–21 (*The Answers Book for Kids Volume 2*)<br>Complete Worksheet 32 (*Teacher Guide*, page 51) | | | |
| | Day 42 | Read pages 22–23 (*The Answers Book for Kids Volume 2*)<br>Complete Worksheet 33 (*Teacher Guide*, page 52) | | | |
| | Day 43 | Read pages 24–25 (*The Answers Book for Kids Volume 2*)<br>Complete Worksheet 34 (*Teacher Guide*, page 53) | | | |
| | Day 44 | Read pages 26–27 (*The Answers Book for Kids Volume 2*)<br>Complete Worksheet 35 (*Teacher Guide*, page 54) | | | |
| | Day 45 | Free day/study day | | | |
| | | First Semester-Second Quarter | | | |
| Week 1 | Day 46 | Read pages 28–29 (*The Answers Book for Kids Volume 2*)<br>Complete Worksheet 36 (*Teacher Guide*, page 55) | | | |
| | Day 47 | Read pages 30–31 (*The Answers Book for Kids Volume 2*)<br>Complete Worksheet 37 (*Teacher Guide*, page 56) | | | |
| | Day 48 | Read pages 32–33 (*The Answers Book for Kids Volume 2*)<br>Complete Worksheet 38 (*Teacher Guide*, page 57) | | | |
| | Day 49 | Read pages 34–35 (*The Answers Book for Kids Volume 2*)<br>Complete Worksheet 39 (*Teacher Guide*, page 58) | | | |
| | Day 50 | Free day/study day | | | |

| Date | Day | Assignment | Due Date | ✓ | Grade |
|---|---|---|---|---|---|
| Week 2 | Day 51 | Read pages 36–37 (*The Answers Book for Kids Volume 2*)<br>Complete Worksheet 40 (*Teacher Guide*, page 59) | | | |
| | Day 52 | Read pages 38–39 (*The Answers Book for Kids Volume 2*)<br>Complete Worksheet 41 (*Teacher Guide*, page 60) | | | |
| | Day 53 | Read pages 40–41 (*The Answers Book for Kids Volume 2*)<br>Complete Worksheet 42 (*Teacher Guide*, page 61) | | | |
| | Day 54 | Read pages 42–43 (*The Answers Book for Kids Volume 2*)<br>Complete Worksheet 43 (*Teacher Guide*, page 62) | | | |
| | Day 55 | Free day/study day | | | |
| Week 3 | Day 56 | Read pages 44–45 (*The Answers Book for Kids Volume 2*)<br>Complete Worksheet 44 (*Teacher Guide*, page 63) | | | |
| | Day 57 | Read pages 46–47 (*The Answers Book for Kids Volume 2*)<br>Complete Worksheet 45 (*Teacher Guide*, page 64) | | | |
| | Day 58 | Quiz 2 (*Teacher Guide*, page 175) | | | |
| | Day 59 | Complete Worksheet 46 (*Teacher Guide*, page 65) | | | |
| | Day 60 | Free day/study day | | | |
| Week 4 | Day 61 | Read pages 4–5 (*The Answers Book for Kids Volume 3*)<br>Complete Worksheet 47 (*Teacher Guide*, page 69) | | | |
| | Day 62 | Read pages 6–7 (*The Answers Book for Kids Volume 3*)<br>Complete Worksheet 48 (*Teacher Guide*, page 70) | | | |
| | Day 63 | Read pages 8–9 (*The Answers Book for Kids Volume 3*)<br>Complete Worksheet 49 (*Teacher Guide*, page 71) | | | |
| | Day 64 | Read pages 10–11 (*The Answers Book for Kids Volume 3*)<br>Complete Worksheet 50 (*Teacher Guide*, page 72) | | | |
| | Day 65 | Free day/study day | | | |
| Week 5 | Day 66 | Read pages 12–13 (*The Answers Book for Kids Volume 3*)<br>Complete Worksheet 51 (*Teacher Guide*, page 73) | | | |
| | Day 67 | Read pages 14–15 (*The Answers Book for Kids Volume 3*)<br>Complete Worksheet 52 (*Teacher Guide*, page 74) | | | |
| | Day 68 | Read pages 16–17 (*The Answers Book for Kids Volume 3*)<br>Complete Worksheet 53 (*Teacher Guide*, page 75) | | | |
| | Day 69 | Read pages 18–19 (*The Answers Book for Kids Volume 3*)<br>Complete Worksheet 54 (*Teacher Guide*, page 76) | | | |
| | Day 70 | Free day/study day | | | |
| Week 6 | Day 71 | Read pages 20–21 (*The Answers Book for Kids Volume 3*)<br>Complete Worksheet 55 (*Teacher Guide*, page 77) | | | |
| | Day 72 | Read pages 22–23 (*The Answers Book for Kids Volume 3*)<br>Complete Worksheet 56 (*Teacher Guide*, page 78) | | | |
| | Day 73 | Read pages 24–25 (*The Answers Book for Kids Volume 3*)<br>Complete Worksheet 57 (*Teacher Guide*, page 79) | | | |
| | Day 74 | Read pages 26–27 (*The Answers Book for Kids Volume 3*)<br>Complete Worksheet 58 (*Teacher Guide*, page 80) | | | |
| | Day 75 | Free day/study day | | | |

| Date | Day | Assignment | Due Date | ✓ | Grade |
|---|---|---|---|---|---|
| Week 7 | Day 76 | Read pages 28–29 (*The Answers Book for Kids Volume 3*)<br>Complete Worksheet 59 (*Teacher Guide*, page 81) | | | |
| | Day 77 | Read pages 30–31 (*The Answers Book for Kids Volume 3*)<br>Complete Worksheet 60 (*Teacher Guide*, page 82) | | | |
| | Day 78 | Read pages 32–33 (*The Answers Book for Kids Volume 3*)<br>Complete Worksheet 61 (*Teacher Guide*, page 83) | | | |
| | Day 79 | Read pages 34–35 (*The Answers Book for Kids Volume 3*)<br>Complete Worksheet 62 (*Teacher Guide*, page 84) | | | |
| | Day 80 | Free day/study day | | | |
| Week 8 | Day 81 | Read pages 36–37 (*The Answers Book for Kids Volume 3*)<br>Complete Worksheet 63 (*Teacher Guide*, page 85) | | | |
| | Day 82 | Read pages 38–39 (*The Answers Book for Kids Volume 3*)<br>Complete Worksheet 64 (*Teacher Guide*, page 86) | | | |
| | Day 83 | Read pages 40–41 (*The Answers Book for Kids Volume 3*)<br>Complete Worksheet 65 (*Teacher Guide*, page 87) | | | |
| | Day 84 | Read pages 42–43 (*The Answers Book for Kids Volume 3*)<br>Complete Worksheet 66 (*Teacher Guide*, page 88) | | | |
| | Day 85 | Free day/study day | | | |
| Week 9 | Day 86 | Read pages 44–45 (*The Answers Book for Kids Volume 3*)<br>Complete Worksheet 67 (*Teacher Guide*, page 89) | | | |
| | Day 87 | Read pages 46–47 (*The Answers Book for Kids Volume 3*)<br>Complete Worksheet 68 (*Teacher Guide*, page 90) | | | |
| | Day 88 | Quiz 3 (*Teacher Guide*, page 177) | | | |
| | Day 89 | Complete Worksheet 69 (*Teacher Guide*, page 91) | | | |
| | Day 90 | Free day/study day | | | |
| | | Mid-Term Grade | | | |

# Second Semester Suggested Daily Schedule

| Date | Day | Assignment | Due Date | ✓ | Grade |
|---|---|---|---|---|---|
| | | Second Semester–Third Quarter | | | |
| Week 1 | Day 91 | Read pages 4–5 (*The Answers Book for Kids Volume 4*)<br>Complete Worksheet 70 (*Teacher Guide*, page 95) | | | |
| | Day 92 | Read pages 6–7 (*The Answers Book for Kids Volume 4*)<br>Complete Worksheet 71 (*Teacher Guide*, page 96) | | | |
| | Day 93 | Read pages 8–9 (*The Answers Book for Kids Volume 4*)<br>Complete Worksheet 72 (*Teacher Guide*, page 97) | | | |
| | Day 94 | Read pages 10–11 (*The Answers Book for Kids Volume 4*)<br>Complete Worksheet 73 (*Teacher Guide*, page 98) | | | |
| | Day 95 | Free day/study day | | | |
| Week 2 | Day 96 | Read pages 12–13 (*The Answers Book for Kids Volume 4*)<br>Complete Worksheet 74 (*Teacher Guide*, page 99) | | | |
| | Day 97 | Read pages 14–15 (*The Answers Book for Kids Volume 4*)<br>Complete Worksheet 75 (*Teacher Guide*, page 100) | | | |
| | Day 98 | Read pages 16–17 (*The Answers Book for Kids Volume 4*)<br>Complete Worksheet 76 (*Teacher Guide*, page 101) | | | |
| | Day 99 | Read pages 18–19 (*The Answers Book for Kids Volume 4*)<br>Complete Worksheet 77 (*Teacher Guide*, page 102) | | | |
| | Day 100 | Free day/study day | | | |
| Week 3 | Day 101 | Read pages 20–21 (*The Answers Book for Kids Volume 4*)<br>Complete Worksheet 78 (*Teacher Guide*, page 103) | | | |
| | Day 102 | Read pages 22–23 (*The Answers Book for Kids Volume 4*)<br>Complete Worksheet 79 (*Teacher Guide*, page 104) | | | |
| | Day 103 | Read pages 24–25 (*The Answers Book for Kids Volume 4*)<br>Complete Worksheet 80 (*Teacher Guide*, page 105) | | | |
| | Day 104 | Read pages 26–27 (*The Answers Book for Kids Volume 4*)<br>Complete Worksheet 81 (*Teacher Guide*, page 106) | | | |
| | Day 105 | Free day/study day | | | |
| Week 4 | Day 106 | Read pages 28–29 (*The Answers Book for Kids Volume 4*)<br>Complete Worksheet 82 (*Teacher Guide*, page 107) | | | |
| | Day 107 | Read pages 30–31 (*The Answers Book for Kids Volume 4*)<br>Complete Worksheet 83 (*Teacher Guide*, page 108) | | | |
| | Day 108 | Read pages 32–33 (*The Answers Book for Kids Volume 4*)<br>Complete Worksheet 84 (*Teacher Guide*, page 109) | | | |
| | Day 109 | Read pages 34–35 (*The Answers Book for Kids Volume 4*)<br>Complete Worksheet 85 (*Teacher Guide*, page 110) | | | |
| | Day 110 | Free day/study day | | | |
| Week 5 | Day 111 | Read pages 36–37 (*The Answers Book for Kids Volume 4*)<br>Complete Worksheet 86 (*Teacher Guide*, page 111) | | | |
| | Day 112 | Read pages 38–39 (*The Answers Book for Kids Volume 4*)<br>Complete Worksheet 87 (*Teacher Guide*, page 112) | | | |
| | Day 113 | Read pages 40–41 (*The Answers Book for Kids Volume 4*)<br>Complete Worksheet 88 (*Teacher Guide*, page 113) | | | |
| | Day 114 | Read pages 42–43 (*The Answers Book for Kids Volume 4*)<br>Complete Worksheet 89 (*Teacher Guide*, page 114) | | | |
| | Day 115 | Free day/study day | | | |

| Date | Day | Assignment | Due Date | ✓ | Grade |
|---|---|---|---|---|---|
| Week 6 | Day 116 | Read pages 44–45 (*The Answers Book for Kids Volume 4*)<br>Complete Worksheet 90 (*Teacher Guide*, page 115) | | | |
| | Day 117 | Read pages 46–47 (*The Answers Book for Kids Volume 4*)<br>Complete Worksheet 91 (*Teacher Guide*, page 116) | | | |
| | Day 118 | Quiz 4 (*Teacher Guide*, page 179) | | | |
| | Day 119 | Complete Worksheet 92 (*Teacher Guide*, page 117) | | | |
| | Day 120 | Free day/study day | | | |
| Week 7 | Day 121 | Read pages 4–5 (*The Answers Book for Kids Volume 5*)<br>Complete Worksheet 93 (*Teacher Guide*, page 121) | | | |
| | Day 122 | Read pages 6–7 (*The Answers Book for Kids Volume 5*)<br>Complete Worksheet 94 (*Teacher Guide*, page 122) | | | |
| | Day 123 | Read pages 8–9 (*The Answers Book for Kids Volume 5*)<br>Complete Worksheet 95 (*Teacher Guide*, page 123) | | | |
| | Day 124 | Read pages 10–11 (*The Answers Book for Kids Volume 5*)<br>Complete Worksheet 96 (*Teacher Guide*, page 124) | | | |
| | Day 125 | Free day/study day | | | |
| Week 8 | Day 126 | Read pages 12–13 (*The Answers Book for Kids Volume 5*)<br>Complete Worksheet 97 (*Teacher Guide*, page 125) | | | |
| | Day 127 | Read pages 14–15 (*The Answers Book for Kids Volume 5*)<br>Complete Worksheet 98 (*Teacher Guide*, page 126) | | | |
| | Day 128 | Read pages 16–17 (*The Answers Book for Kids Volume 5*)<br>Complete Worksheet 99 (*Teacher Guide*, page 127) | | | |
| | Day 129 | Read pages 18–19 (*The Answers Book for Kids Volume 5*)<br>Complete Worksheet 100 (*Teacher Guide*, page 128) | | | |
| | Day 130 | Free day/study day | | | |
| Week 9 | Day 131 | Read pages 20–21 (*The Answers Book for Kids Volume 5*)<br>Complete Worksheet 101 (*Teacher Guide*, page 129) | | | |
| | Day 132 | Read pages 22–23 (*The Answers Book for Kids Volume 5*)<br>Complete Worksheet 102 (*Teacher Guide*, page 130) | | | |
| | Day 133 | Read pages 24–25 (*The Answers Book for Kids Volume 5*)<br>Complete Worksheet 103 (*Teacher Guide*, page 131) | | | |
| | Day 134 | Read pages 26–27 (*The Answers Book for Kids Volume 5*)<br>Complete Worksheet 104 (*Teacher Guide*, page 132) | | | |
| | Day 135 | Free day/study day | | | |
| Second Semester-Fourth Quarter | | | | | |
| Week 1 | Day 136 | Read pages 28–29 (*The Answers Book for Kids Volume 5*)<br>Complete Worksheet 105 (*Teacher Guide*, page 133) | | | |
| | Day 137 | Read pages 30–31 (*The Answers Book for Kids Volume 5*)<br>Complete Worksheet 106 (*Teacher Guide*, page 134) | | | |
| | Day 138 | Read pages 32–33 (*The Answers Book for Kids Volume 5*)<br>Complete Worksheet 107 (*Teacher Guide*, page 135) | | | |
| | Day 139 | Read pages 34–35 (*The Answers Book for Kids Volume 5*)<br>Complete Worksheet 108 (*Teacher Guide*, page 136) | | | |
| | Day 140 | Free day/study day | | | |

| Date | Day | Assignment | Due Date | ✓ | Grade |
|---|---|---|---|---|---|
| Week 2 | Day 141 | Read pages 36–37 (*The Answers Book for Kids Volume 5*)<br>Complete Worksheet 109 (*Teacher Guide*, page 137) | | | |
| | Day 142 | Read pages 38–39 (*The Answers Book for Kids Volume 5*)<br>Complete Worksheet 110 (*Teacher Guide*, page 138) | | | |
| | Day 143 | Read pages 40–41 (*The Answers Book for Kids Volume 5*)<br>Complete Worksheet 111 (*Teacher Guide*, page 139) | | | |
| | Day 144 | Read pages 42–43 (*The Answers Book for Kids Volume 5*)<br>Complete Worksheet 112 (*Teacher Guide*, page 140) | | | |
| | Day 145 | Free day/study day | | | |
| Week 3 | Day 146 | Read pages 44–45 (*The Answers Book for Kids Volume 5*)<br>Complete Worksheet 113 (*Teacher Guide*, page 141) | | | |
| | Day 147 | Read pages 46–47 (*The Answers Book for Kids Volume 5*)<br>Complete Worksheet 114 (*Teacher Guide*, page 142) | | | |
| | Day 148 | Quiz 5 (*Teacher Guide*, page 181) | | | |
| | Day 149 | Complete Worksheet 115 (*Teacher Guide*, page 143) | | | |
| | Day 150 | Free day/study day | | | |
| Week 4 | Day 151 | Read pages 4–5 (*The Answers Book for Kids Volume 6*)<br>Complete Worksheet 116 (*Teacher Guide*, page 147) | | | |
| | Day 152 | Read pages 6–7 (*The Answers Book for Kids Volume 6*)<br>Complete Worksheet 117 (*Teacher Guide*, page 148) | | | |
| | Day 153 | Read pages 8–9 (*The Answers Book for Kids Volume 6*)<br>Complete Worksheet 118 (*Teacher Guide*, page 149) | | | |
| | Day 154 | Read pages 10–11 (*The Answers Book for Kids Volume 6*)<br>Complete Worksheet 119 (*Teacher Guide*, page 150) | | | |
| | Day 155 | Free day/study day | | | |
| Week 5 | Day 156 | Read pages 12–13 (*The Answers Book for Kids Volume 6*)<br>Complete Worksheet 120 (*Teacher Guide*, page 151) | | | |
| | Day 157 | Read pages 14–15 (*The Answers Book for Kids Volume 6*)<br>Complete Worksheet 121 (*Teacher Guide*, page 152) | | | |
| | Day 158 | Read pages 16–17 (*The Answers Book for Kids Volume 6*)<br>Complete Worksheet 122 (*Teacher Guide*, page 153) | | | |
| | Day 159 | Read pages 18–19 (*The Answers Book for Kids Volume 6*)<br>Complete Worksheet 123 (*Teacher Guide*, page 154) | | | |
| | Day 160 | Free day/study day | | | |
| Week 6 | Day 161 | Read pages 20–21 (*The Answers Book for Kids Volume 6*)<br>Complete Worksheet 124 (*Teacher Guide*, page 155) | | | |
| | Day 162 | Read pages 22–23 (*The Answers Book for Kids Volume 6*)<br>Complete Worksheet 125 (*Teacher Guide*, page 156) | | | |
| | Day 163 | Read pages 24–25 (*The Answers Book for Kids Volume 6*)<br>Complete Worksheet 126 (*Teacher Guide*, page 157) | | | |
| | Day 164 | Read pages 26–27 (*The Answers Book for Kids Volume 6*)<br>Complete Worksheet 127 (*Teacher Guide*, page 158) | | | |
| | Day 165 | Free day/study day | | | |

| Date | Day | Assignment | Due Date | ✓ | Grade |
|---|---|---|---|---|---|
| Week 7 | Day 166 | Read pages 28–29 (*The Answers Book for Kids Volume 6*)<br>Complete Worksheet 128 (*Teacher Guide*, page 159) | | | |
| | Day 167 | Read pages 30–31 (*The Answers Book for Kids Volume 6*)<br>Complete Worksheet 129 (*Teacher Guide*, page 160) | | | |
| | Day 168 | Read pages 32–33 (*The Answers Book for Kids Volume 6*)<br>Complete Worksheet 130 (*Teacher Guide*, page 161) | | | |
| | Day 169 | Read pages 34–35 (*The Answers Book for Kids Volume 6*)<br>Complete Worksheet 131 (*Teacher Guide*, page 162) | | | |
| | Day 170 | Free day/study day | | | |
| Week 8 | Day 171 | Read pages 36–37 (*The Answers Book for Kids Volume 6*)<br>Complete Worksheet 132 (*Teacher Guide*, page 163) | | | |
| | Day 172 | Read pages 38–39 (*The Answers Book for Kids Volume 6*)<br>Complete Worksheet 133 (*Teacher Guide*, page 164) | | | |
| | Day 173 | Read pages 40–41 (*The Answers Book for Kids Volume 6*)<br>Complete Worksheet 134 (*Teacher Guide*, page 165) | | | |
| | Day 174 | Read pages 42–43 (*The Answers Book for Kids Volume 6*)<br>Complete Worksheet 135 (*Teacher Guide*, page 166) | | | |
| | Day 175 | Free day/study day | | | |
| Week 9 | Day 176 | Read pages 44–45 (*The Answers Book for Kids Volume 6*)<br>Complete Worksheet 136 (*Teacher Guide*, page 167) | | | |
| | Day 177 | Read pages 46–47 (*The Answers Book for Kids Volume 6*)<br>Complete Worksheet 137 (*Teacher Guide*, page 168) | | | |
| | Day 178 | Quiz 6 (*Teacher Guide*, page 183) | | | |
| | Day 179 | Complete Worksheet 138 (*Teacher Guide*, page 169) | | | |
| | Day 180 | Free day/study day | | | |
| | | Final Grade | | | |

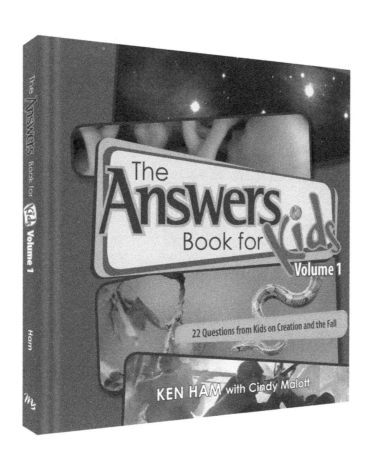

Worksheets

for Use with

*The Answers Book for Kids Volume 1*

| The Answers Book for Kids Volume 1 | Pages 4–5 | Day 1 | Worksheet 1 | Name |

**?** When did time begin?

✝ Study and memorize the verse from today (Genesis 1:1), and recite it to your teacher.

✏ Write out the following passages from your Bible: 2 Peter 3:8; Revelation 1:8.

 Write a short note to a friend about what you studied today.

| The Answers Book for Kids Volume 1 | Pages 6–7 | Day 2 | Worksheet 2 | Name |

**?** How did God create everything from nothing?

___

**✝** Study and memorize the verse from today (Hebrews 11:3), and recite it to your teacher.

**✎** Write out the following passages from your Bible: Exodus 20:11; Genesis 1:14–15.

___

Discuss the answer of today's question with your teacher and why you believe it's important to know.

| The Answers Book for Kids Volume 1 | Pages 8–9 | Day 3 | Worksheet 3 | Name |

**?** Did Adam and Eve have bellybuttons?

**✝** Study and memorize the verses from today (Genesis 2:7, 22), and recite them to your teacher.

**✎** Write out the following passage from your Bible: Genesis 2:5–7.

**☺** Write or discuss a question with your teacher that you or a friend has had about God or His world.

Elementary Apologetics // 19

| The Answers Book for Kids Volume 1 | Pages 10–11 | Day 4 | Worksheet 4 | Name |

**?** Where is the Garden of Eden?

___

**†** Study and memorize the verses from today (Genesis 2:10–14), and recite them to your teacher.

**✎** Write out the following passage from your Bible: Genesis 7:23.

___

Draw a picture related to your favorite question of the week and share the meaning with your teacher.

| The Answers Book for Kids Volume 1 | Pages 12–13 | Day 6 | Worksheet 5 | Name |

**?** Does Genesis 1:1–2 refer to the first day?

Study and memorize the verse from today (Genesis 1:5), and recite it to your teacher.

Write out the following passage from your Bible: Genesis 1:1–5.

Write a short note to a friend about what you studied today.

| The Answers Book for Kids Volume 1 | Pages 14–15 | Day 7 | Worksheet 6 | Name |

**?** When God created the earth, were the trees fully grown, or were they baby trees? If they were full grown, did they have growth rings?

___

___

___

___

**✝** Study and memorize the verse from today (Genesis 1:12), and recite it to your teacher.

**✏** Write out the following passage from your Bible: Genesis 1:29–31.

___

___

___

___

___

___

___

**👥** Discuss the answer of today's question with your teacher and why you believe it's important to know.

22 // Elementary Apologetics

| | The Answers Book for Kids Volume 1 | Pages 16–17 | Day 8 | Worksheet 7 | Name |

**?** Why did God make a week seven days long?

___

**†** Study and memorize the verse from today (Exodus 20:11), and recite it to your teacher.

**✎** Write out the following passage from your Bible: Exodus 16:25–27.

___

**☺** Write or discuss a question with your teacher that you or a friend has had about God or His world.

| The Answers Book for Kids Volume 1 | Pages 18–19 | Day 9 | Worksheet 8 | Name |

**?** Why was the first person that God created a boy?

___

**✝** Study and memorize the verse from today (Genesis 2:18), and recite it to your teacher.

**✎** Write out the following passage from your Bible: Ephesians 5:22–25.

___

Draw a picture related to your favorite question of the week and share the meaning with your teacher.

| The Answers Book for Kids Volume 1 | Pages 20–21 | Day 11 | Worksheet 9 | Name |

**?** Why did God let Adam name the animals? Why didn't He name them Himself?

___

Study and memorize the verse from today (Genesis 2:18), and recite it to your teacher.

Write out the following passage from your Bible: Genesis 2:19–20.

___

Write a short note to a friend about what you studied today.

| The Answers Book for Kids Volume 1 | Pages 22–23 | Day 12 | Worksheet 10 | Name |

**?** Did Adam give each of the animals the names we call them today?

___

___

___

___

**✝** Study and memorize the verse from today (Genesis 2:20), and recite it to your teacher.

**✏** Write out the following passage from your Bible: Genesis 11:7–9.

___

___

___

___

___

___

___

**☺** Discuss the answer of today's question with your teacher and why you believe it's important to know.

| The Answers Book for Kids Volume 1 | Pages 24–25 | Day 13 | Worksheet 11 | Name |

**?** How long did it take Adam to name the animals?

_____

_____

_____

_____

_____

**✝** Study and memorize the verse from today (Genesis 2:19), and recite it to your teacher.

**✎** Write out the following passage from your Bible: Genesis 2:18–20.

_____

_____

_____

_____

_____

_____

_____

_____

_____

_____

Write or discuss a question with your teacher that you or a friend has had about God or His world.

| The Answers Book for Kids Volume 1 | Pages 26–27 | Day 14 | Worksheet 12 | Name |

**?** The serpent talked to Eve, so why can't snakes talk today?

_____

_____

_____

_____

**✝** Study and memorize the verse from today (Numbers 22:30), and recite it to your teacher.

**✎** Write out the following passage from your Bible: Genesis 3:1–3.

_____

_____

_____

_____

_____

_____

_____

Draw a picture related to your favorite question of the week and share the meaning with your teacher.

| The Answers Book for Kids Volume 1 | Pages 28–29 | Day 16 | Worksheet 13 | Name |

**?** Why did God put the tree in the Garden of Eden if He didn't want Adam and Eve to eat the fruit from it?

___

**†** Study and memorize the verse from today (Genesis 2:17), and recite it to your teacher.

**✏** Write out the following passages from your Bible: John 3:16; Romans 5:12.

___

**👥** Write a short note to a friend about what you studied today.

| The Answers Book for Kids Volume 1 | Pages 30–31 | Day 17 | Worksheet 14 | Name |

**?** If all that God created was good, how could Satan be bad?

_____

_____

_____

_____

✝ Study and memorize the verse from today (Genesis 1:31), and recite it to your teacher.

✏ Write out the following passages from your Bible: Isaiah 14:13; James 1:13–15.

_____

_____

_____

_____

_____

_____

_____

_____

👥 Discuss the answer of today's question with your teacher and why you believe it's important to know.

30 // Elementary Apologetics

| The Answers Book for Kids Volume 1 | Pages 32–33 | Day 18 | Worksheet 15 | Name |

**?** Who was Cain's wife? Why doesn't the Bible mention her birth if she was Eve's baby?

**†** Study and memorize the verse from today (Genesis 5:4), and recite it to your teacher.

**✎** Write out the following passages from your Bible: Genesis 2:24; Genesis 20:12; Leviticus 18:6.

**☺** Write or discuss a question with your teacher that you or a friend has had about God or His world.

Elementary Apologetics

| The Answers Book for Kids Volume 1 | Pages 34–35 | Day 19 | Worksheet 16 | Name |

**?** Did bumblebees have stingers before Adam and Eve sinned?

_____
_____
_____
_____

**†** Study and memorize the verse from today (Romans 8:22), and recite it to your teacher.

**✎** Write out the following passage from your Bible: Genesis 3:17–18.

_____
_____
_____
_____
_____
_____
_____

**☺** Draw a picture related to your favorite question of the week and share the meaning with your teacher.

| The Answers Book for Kids Volume 1 | Pages 36–37 | Day 21 | Worksheet 17 | Name |

**?** How long were Adam and Eve in the Garden of Eden before they sinned?

**†** Study and memorize the verse from today (Genesis 1:28), and recite it to your teacher.

**✎** Write out the following passages from your Bible: Romans 3:23; Romans 5:12.

**☺** Write a short note to a friend about what you studied today.

| | *The Answers Book for Kids Volume 1* | Pages 38–39 | Day 22 | Worksheet 18 | Name |

**?** When were the other planets created?

___

**✝** Study and memorize the verses from today (Genesis 1:16, 19), and recite them to your teacher.

**✎** Write out the following passages from your Bible: Psalm 19:1; Psalm 33:6.

___

**☺** Discuss the answer of today's question with your teacher and why you believe it's important to know.

34 **//** Elementary Apologetics

| The Answers Book for Kids Volume 1 | Pages 40–41 | Day 23 | Worksheet 19 | Name |

**?** If God created the world 6,000 years ago or so, why are stars millions of light years away?

**✝** Study and memorize the verse from today (Psalm 19:1), and recite it to your teacher.

**✎** Write out the following passages from your Bible: Psalm 50:6; Psalm 147:4; Isaiah 40:26.

**☺** Write or discuss a question with your teacher that you or a friend has had about God or His world.

Elementary Apologetics

| | The Answers Book for Kids Volume 1 | Pages 42–43 | Day 24 | Worksheet 20 | Name |

**?** What is evolution?

_____

_____

_____

_____

**✝** Study and memorize the verse from today (Genesis 1:21), and recite it to your teacher.

**✎** Write out the following passage from your Bible: Genesis 1:20–21.

_____

_____

_____

_____

_____

_____

_____

**☺** Draw a picture related to your favorite question of the week and share the meaning with your teacher.

36 // Elementary Apologetics

| The Answers Book for Kids Volume 1 | Pages 44–45 | Day 26 | Worksheet 21 | Name |

**?** Why do evolutionists trust their beliefs and not Christ?

**✝** Study and memorize the verse from today (2 Peter 3:5), and recite it to your teacher.

**✎** Write out the following passage from your Bible: Genesis 1:24–25.

**☺** Write a short note to a friend about what you studied today.

| | *The Answers Book for Kids Volume 1* | Pages 46–47 | Day 27 | Worksheet 22 | Name |

**?** Did God use the same design for humans as for monkeys?

---

**✝** Study and memorize the verse from today (Genesis 1:26), and recite it to your teacher.

---

**✎** Write out the following passages from your Bible: Psalm 104:24; 1 John 3:1; John 1:12.

---

**👥** Discuss the answer of today's question with your teacher and why you believe it's important to know.

| The Answers Book for Kids Volume 1 | End of Book | Day 29 | Worksheet 23 | Name |

Match the passage with the biblical book, chapter, and verse from the verses in your book.

Genesis 1:1     Genesis 1:21     Genesis 1:31     Genesis 2:18     Psalm 19:1
Genesis 1:5     Genesis 1:26     Genesis 2:17     Exodus 20:11     Romans 8:22

1. _____ For in six days the LORD made the heavens and the earth, the sea, and all that is in them, and rested the seventh day. Therefore the LORD blessed the Sabbath day and hallowed it.

2. _____ So God created great sea creatures and every living thing that moves, with which the waters abounded, according to their kind, and every winged bird according to its kind. And God saw that it was good.

3. _____ The heavens declare the glory of God; and the firmament shows His handiwork.

4. _____ Then God saw everything that He had made, and indeed it was very good. So the evening and the morning were the sixth day.

5. _____ In the beginning God created the heavens and the earth.

6. _____ For we know that the whole creation groans and labors with birth pangs together until now.

7. _____ So the evening and the morning were the first day.

8. _____ ... but of the tree of the knowledge of good and evil you shall not eat, for in the day that you eat of it you shall surely die.

9. _____ Then God said, "Let Us make man in Our image, according to Our likeness."

10. _____ And the Lord God said, "It is not good that man should be alone; I will make him a helper comparable to him."

Elementary Apologetics

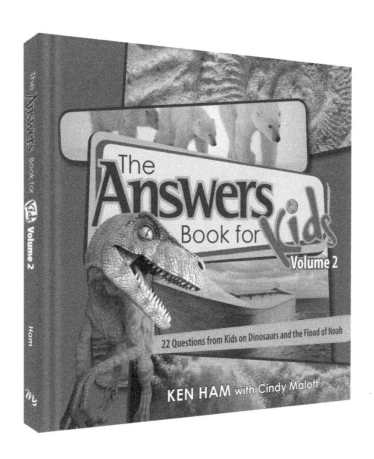

Worksheets

for Use with

*The Answers Book for Kids Volume 2*

| The Answers Book for Kids Volume 2 | Pages 4–5 | Day 31 | Worksheet 24 | Name |

**?** Were people different before the Flood than they are today?

**✝** Study and memorize the verses from today (Genesis 11:1, 7), and recite them to your teacher.

**✎** Write out the following passage from your Bible: Genesis 11:6–8.

**☺** Write a short note to a friend about what you studied today.

Elementary Apologetics

| The Answers Book for Kids Volume 2 | Pages 6–7 | Day 32 | Worksheet 25 | Name |

**?** Did Noah take dinosaurs on the ark?

**✝** Study and memorize the verse from today (Genesis 6:19), and recite it to your teacher.

**✎** Write out the following passage from your Bible: Genesis 6:19–20.

**☺** Discuss the answer of today's question with your teacher and why you believe it's important to know.

| | The Answers Book for Kids Volume 2 | Pages 8–9 | Day 33 | Worksheet 26 | Name |

**?** How did all the dinosaurs fit on the ark?

**✝** Study and memorize the verse from today (Genesis 6:15), and recite it to your teacher.

**✎** Write out the following passages from your Bible: Genesis 1:25; Genesis 7:14.

**☺** Write or discuss a question with your teacher that you or a friend has had about God or His world.

Elementary Apologetics 45

| The Answers Book for Kids Volume 2 | Pages 10–11 | Day 34 | Worksheet 27 | Name |

**?** How did Noah get two of every sea animal on the ark?

**✝** Study and memorize the verse from today (Genesis 6:20), and recite it to your teacher.

**✎** Write out the following passages from your Bible: Genesis 6:17; Genesis 7:15; Genesis 7:22.

**☺** Draw a picture related to your favorite question of the week and share the meaning with your teacher.

| The Answers Book for Kids Volume 2 | Pages 12–13 | Day 36 | Worksheet 28 | Name |

**?** Did Noah have to estimate how much food to gather, or did God tell him?

_____

_____

_____

_____

**✝** Study and memorize the verse from today (Genesis 6:21), and recite it to your teacher.

**✏** Write out the following passages from your Bible: Genesis 7:5; Genesis 8:1.

_____

_____

_____

_____

_____

_____

_____

_____

**☺** Write a short note to a friend about what you studied today.

Elementary Apologetics

| The Answers Book for Kids Volume 2 | Pages 14–15 | Day 37 | Worksheet 29 | Name |

**?** How did Noah keep the animals on the ark from eating each other and his family?

_____

_____

_____

_____

**✝** Study and memorize the verse from today (Genesis 8:1), and recite it to your teacher.

**✎** Write out the following passages from your Bible: Genesis 1:29–30; Genesis 9:3.

_____

_____

_____

_____

_____

_____

_____

 Discuss the answer of today's question with your teacher and why you believe it's important to know.

| The Answers Book for Kids Volume 2 | Pages 16–17 | Day 38 | Worksheet 30 | Name |

**?** Why did God make meat-eating animals? Why are they not still plant-eaters?

___

**†** Study and memorize the verse from today (Genesis 1:30), and recite it to your teacher.

**✎** Write out the following passages from your Bible: Romans 6:23; Revelation 21:4.

___

Write or discuss a question with your teacher that you or a friend has had about God or His world.

| The Answers Book for Kids Volume 2 | Pages 18–19 | Day 39 | Worksheet 31 | Name |

**?** Why did God allow some creatures to go extinct?

___

**✝** Study and memorize the verse from today (Genesis 2:17), and recite it to your teacher.

**✏** Write out the following passages from your Bible: Genesis 1:31; Romans 5:12; Psalm 33:20–22.

___

Draw a picture related to your favorite question of the week and share the meaning with your teacher.

| The Answers Book for Kids Volume 2 | Pages 20–21 | Day 41 | Worksheet 32 | Name |

**?** What happened to the ark once Noah, his family, and the animals got off?

**✝** Study and memorize the verses from today (Genesis 8:15–16), and recite them to your teacher.

**✎** Write out the following passage from your Bible: Genesis 8:13–16.

**☺** Write a short note to a friend about what you studied today.

Elementary Apologetics // 51

| The Answers Book for Kids Volume 2 | Pages 22–23 | Day 42 | Worksheet 33 | Name |

**?** After the Flood, were there any buildings left?

___

**✝** Study and memorize the verse from today (Genesis 6:7), and recite it to your teacher.

**✎** Write out the following passages from your Bible: Genesis 7:4; Luke 17:27.

___

**👧👦** Discuss the answer of today's question with your teacher and why you believe it's important to know.

| | *The Answers Book for Kids Volume 2* | Pages 24–25 | Day 43 | Worksheet 34 | Name |

**?** Did we use dinosaurs for transportation?

**✝** Study and memorize the verse from today (James 3:7), and recite it to your teacher.

**✏** Write out the following passage from your Bible: Genesis 2:19–20.

**☺** Write or discuss a question with your teacher that you or a friend has had about God or His world.

Elementary Apologetics // 53

| *The Answers Book for Kids Volume 2* | Pages 26–27 | Day 44 | Worksheet 35 | Name |

**?** Did Noah have to search for all the animals, or did they come by themselves? How did they know they had to come to the ark?

___

___

___

___

**✝** Study and memorize the verse from today (Genesis 6:20), and recite it to your teacher.

**✎** Write out the following passages from your Bible: Genesis 6:20; Genesis 7:8–9.

___

___

___

___

___

___

___

**☺** Draw a picture related to your favorite question of the week and share the meaning with your teacher.

| The Answers Book for Kids Volume 2 | Pages 28–29 | Day 46 | Worksheet 36 | Name |

**?** Where did all the water go after the Flood?

_____

_____

_____

_____

Study and memorize the verse from today (Psalm 104:8), and recite it to your teacher.

Write out the following passages from your Bible: Genesis 8:21; Genesis 9:11.

_____

_____

_____

_____

_____

_____

_____

_____

Write a short note to a friend about what you studied today.

Elementary Apologetics // 55

| | *The Answers Book for Kids Volume 2* | Pages 30–31 | Day 47 | Worksheet 37 | Name |

**?** Why aren't there fossils of humans from Noah's flood?

_____

_____

_____

_____

**✝** Study and memorize the verse from today (Genesis 6:7), and recite it to your teacher.

**✎** Write out the following passages from your Bible: Matthew 24:39; Psalm 29:10.

_____

_____

_____

_____

_____

_____

_____

**☺** Discuss the answer of today's question with your teacher and why you believe it's important to know.

**Elementary Apologetics**

| | The Answers Book for Kids Volume 2 | Pages 32–33 | Day 48 | Worksheet 38 | Name |

**?** Are dinosaurs still alive today? Has anybody ever taken a picture of a dinosaur?

___

**†** Study and memorize the verses from today (Job 40:15–18), and recite them to your teacher.

**✎** Write out the following passages from your Bible: Isaiah 14:29; Job 41:1.

___

 Write or discuss a question with your teacher that you or a friend has had about God or His world.

| The Answers Book for Kids Volume 2 | Pages 34–35 | Day 49 | Worksheet 39 | Name |

**?** Did a meteor really kill all the dinosaurs? Where did all the dinosaurs go?

___

**✝** Study and memorize the verse from today (Genesis 8:17), and recite it to your teacher.

**✎** Write out the following passages from your Bible: Genesis 10:9; Genesis 8:19.

___

Draw a picture related to your favorite question of the week and share the meaning with your teacher.

| The Answers Book for Kids Volume 2 | Pages 36–37 | Day 51 | Worksheet 40 | Name |

**?** Were there people alive when the dinosaurs roamed the earth?

**†** Study and memorize the verses from today (Genesis 1:25, 26, 31), and recite them to your teacher.

**✎** Write out the following passage from your Bible: Job 40:15–18.

**☺** Write a short note to a friend about what you studied today.

Elementary Apologetics // 59

| | The Answers Book for Kids Volume 2 | Pages 38–39 | Day 52 | Worksheet 41 | Name |

**?** Are dinosaurs related to birds?

**✝** Study and memorize the verses from today (Genesis 1:20, 23), and recite them to your teacher.

**✏** Write out the following passages from your Bible: Genesis 1:22; Genesis 1:28.

**☺** Discuss the answer of today's question with your teacher and why you believe it's important to know.

| The Answers Book for Kids Volume 2 | Pages 40–41 | Day 53 | Worksheet 42 | Name |

**How could Noah's children fill the earth?**

Study and memorize the verse from today (Genesis 9:1), and recite it to your teacher.

Write out the following passages from your Bible: Genesis 1:28; Genesis 9:7.

Write or discuss a question with your teacher that you or a friend has had about God or His world.

| | *The Answers Book for Kids Volume 2* | Pages 42–43 | Day 54 | Worksheet 43 | Name |

**?** The books we get from the library state that caves and cave formations took thousands of years to form. We wondered how long they really took and if or how they were related to the world-wide flood.

_____

_____

_____

_____

**✝** Study and memorize the verse from today (Job 30:6), and recite it to your teacher.

**✎** Write out the following passages from your Bible: Genesis 8:3; 1 Kings 18:13; John 11:38.

_____

_____

_____

_____

_____

_____

_____

**☺** Draw a picture related to your favorite question of the week and share the meaning with your teacher.

| The Answers Book for Kids Volume 2 | Pages 44–45 | Day 56 | Worksheet 44 | Name |

**?** Why doesn't the Bible tell us about the Ice Age?

**✝** Study and memorize the verse from today (Genesis 7:11), and recite it to your teacher.

**✏** Write out the following passage from your Bible: Job 37:9–10.

 Write a short note to a friend about what you studied today.

| The Answers Book for Kids Volume 2 | Pages 46–47 | Day 57 | Worksheet 45 | Name |

? Since we all came from Adam and Eve, shouldn't we all have the same color of skin?

✝ Study and memorize the verse from today (Acts 17:26), and recite it to your teacher.

✏ Write out the following passages from your Bible: Genesis 9:19; Genesis 11:9.

👥 Discuss the answer of today's question with your teacher and why you believe it's important to know.

| The Answers Book for Kids Volume 2 | End of Book | Day 59 | Worksheet 46 | Name |

 Match the passage with the biblical book, chapter, and verse from the verses in your book.

Genesis 1:20, 23   Genesis 6:19   Genesis 8:1   Genesis 11:1, 7   Job 40:15
Genesis 6:7        Genesis 6:21   Genesis 9:1   Job 30:6          Psalm 104:8 ESV

1. _____ Now the whole earth had one language and one speech. . . . "Come, let Us go down and there confuse their language, that they may not understand one another's speech."

2. _____ Look now at the behemoth, which I made along with you.

3. _____ And of every living thing of all flesh you shall bring two of every sort into the ark, to keep them alive with you; they shall be male and female.

4. _____ They had to live in the clefts of the valleys, In caves of the earth and the rocks.

5. _____ Then God said, ". . . let birds fly above the earth across the face of the firmament of the heavens." . . . So the evening and the morning were the fifth day.

6. _____ So the LORD said, "I will destroy man whom I have created from the face of the earth, both man and beast, creeping thing and birds of the air."

7. _____ The mountains rose, the valleys sank down to the place that you appointed for them.

8. _____ And you shall take for yourself of all food that is eaten, and you shall gather it to yourself; and it shall be food for you and for them.

9. _____ Then God remembered Noah, and every living thing, and all the animals that were with him in the ark. And God made a wind to pass over the earth, and the waters subsided.

10. _____ So God blessed Noah and his sons, and said to them: "Be fruitful and multiply, and fill the earth."

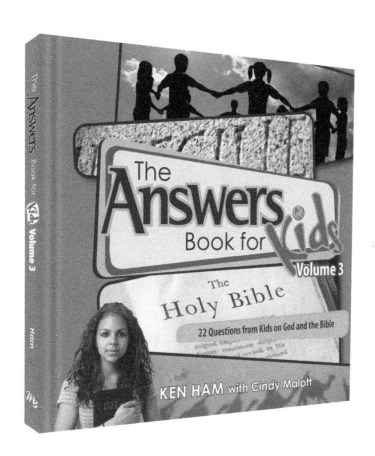

**Worksheets**

**for Use with**

*The Answers Book for Kids Volume 3*

| The Answers Book for Kids Volume 3 | Pages 4–5 | Day 61 | Worksheet 47 | Name |

**?** I don't know if I believe in God because, I mean, who made God anyway?

___

**✝** Study and memorize the verse from today (Revelation 1:8), and recite it to your teacher.

**✎** Write out the following passages from your Bible: Genesis 1:1; Psalm 19:1; Revelation 4:11.

___

**☺** Write a short note to a friend about what you studied today.

Elementary Apologetics

| The Answers Book for Kids Volume 3 | Pages 6–7 | Day 62 | Worksheet 48 | Name |

**?** What does God look like?

_____

_____

_____

_____

_____

**✝** Study and memorize the verse from today (1 Timothy 6:16), and recite it to your teacher.

**✎** Write out the following passages from your Bible: Romans 3:23; John 4:24; John 3:16; 2 Corinthians 4:6.

_____

_____

_____

_____

_____

_____

_____

_____

**👥** Discuss the answer of today's question with your teacher and why you believe it's important to know.

| *The Answers Book for Kids Volume 3* | Pages 8–9 | Day 63 | Worksheet 49 | Name |

**Where is God? Why can't I see Him?**

___

Study and memorize the verse from today (Exodus 33:20), and recite it to your teacher.

Write out the following passage from your Bible: Psalm 139:1–5.

___

 Write or discuss a question with your teacher that you or a friend has had about God or His world.

Elementary Apologetics // 71

| The Answers Book for Kids Volume 3 | Pages 10–11 | Day 64 | Worksheet 50 | Name |

**How big is God?**

___

Study and memorize the verse from today (Jeremiah 23:24), and recite it to your teacher.

Write out the following passages from your Bible: Genesis 1:1; Jeremiah 10:6; Psalm 86:8.

___

Draw a picture related to your favorite question of the week and share the meaning with your teacher.

| The Answers Book for Kids Volume 3 | Pages 12–13 | Day 66 | Worksheet 51 | Name |

**?** How does God get His power? Where does He get it from?

___

Study and memorize the verse from today (Jeremiah 32:17), and recite it to your teacher.

___

Write out the following passages from your Bible: Psalm 147:5; Nehemiah 9:6; Mark 10:27.

___

Write a short note to a friend about what you studied today.

| | The Answers Book for Kids Volume 3 | Pages 14–15 | Day 67 | Worksheet 52 | Name |

**?** Does God laugh?

**†** Study and memorize the verse from today (Psalm 37:13), and recite it to your teacher.

**✎** Write out the following passages from your Bible: Genesis 1:27; Isaiah 62:5; Psalm 2:4; Proverbs 1:26; Psalm 16:11.

Discuss the answer of today's question with your teacher and why you believe it's important to know.

Elementary Apologetics

| The Answers Book for Kids Volume 3 | Pages 16–17 | Day 68 | Worksheet 53 | Name |

**?** How does God know something before it happens?

**✝** Study and memorize the verse from today (2 Peter 3:8), and recite it to your teacher.

**✏** Write out the following passages from your Bible: Isaiah 46:9–10.

**☺** Write or discuss a question with your teacher that you or a friend has had about God or His world.

Elementary Apologetics // 75

**?** How could God be Jesus and Jesus be God? How can they be the same, but different?

_____

_____

_____

_____

Study and memorize the verses from today (John 1:1–3), and recite them to your teacher.

Write out the following passages from your Bible: Deuteronomy 6:4; Colossians 1:16; John 1:1.

_____

_____

_____

_____

_____

_____

 Draw a picture related to your favorite question of the week and share the meaning with your teacher.

| The Answers Book for Kids Volume 3 | Pages 20–21 | Day 71 | Worksheet 55 | Name |

**?** Is the Holy Spirit even with God?

___

Study and memorize the verse from today (John 14:16), and recite it to your teacher.

Write out the following passage from your Bible: John 15:26.

___

Write a short note to a friend about what you studied today.

Elementary Apologetics // 77

| The Answers Book for Kids Volume 3 | Pages 22–23 | Day 72 | Worksheet 56 | Name |

**?** Why can't I hear God talking to me?

___

**✝** Study and memorize the verses from today (Hebrews 1:1–2), and recite them to your teacher.

**✎** Write out the following passages from your Bible: 2 Timothy 3:16–17; Proverbs 30:5–6.

___

 Discuss the answer of today's question with your teacher and why you believe it's important to know.

| The Answers Book for Kids Volume 3 | Pages 24–25 | Day 73 | Worksheet 57 | Name |

**?** How do we know that God really answers prayers? Couldn't it be just a coincidence?

___

**✝** Study and memorize the verse from today (Matthew 6:6), and recite it to your teacher.

**✎** Write out the following passages from your Bible: Romans 8:28; Job 42:2; Mark 1:35; Hebrews 11:6.

___

**👧👦** Write or discuss a question with your teacher that you or a friend has had about God or His world.

Elementary Apologetics // 79

| *The Answers Book for Kids Volume 3* | Pages 26–27 | Day 74 | Worksheet 58 | Name |

**?** Why did God create sin?

---

**✝** Study and memorize the verse from today (Romans 5:12), and recite it to your teacher.

**✏** Write out the following passages from your Bible: Romans 3:23; Romans 6:23; John 3:16.

---

Draw a picture related to your favorite question of the week and share the meaning with your teacher.

| *The Answers Book for Kids Volume 3* | Pages 28–29 | Day 76 | Worksheet 59 | Name |

**?** In the Bible, God is a God of second chances. God gives us a second chance when we sin. So, why didn't God give Adam and Eve a second chance in the Garden of Eden even though they sinned?

___

Study and memorize the verses from today (Ephesians 2:8–9), and recite them to your teacher.

Write out the following passages from your Bible: Job 42:2; Acts 4:12.

___

Write a short note to a friend about what you studied today.

| | The Answers Book for Kids Volume 3 | Pages 30–31 | Day 77 | Worksheet 60 | Name |

**?** Why did God allow the Israelites to kill people?

___

___

___

___

**†** Study and memorize the verse from today (Genesis 6:5), and recite it to your teacher.

**✏** Write out the following passages from your Bible: Psalm 14:2–3; 2 Peter 3:7; Romans 10:13.

___

___

___

___

___

___

___

___

**☺** Discuss the answer of today's question with your teacher and why you believe it's important to know.

| *The Answers Book for Kids Volume 3* | Pages 32–33 | Day 78 | Worksheet 61 | Name |

**Why did God create us?**

---

Study and memorize the verse from today (Romans 11:36), and recite it to your teacher.

Write out the following passages from your Bible: Zephaniah 3:17; 1 Corinthians 10:31; 1 Peter 4:11.

---

Write or discuss a question with your teacher that you or a friend has had about God or His world.

| The Answers Book for Kids Volume 3 | Pages 34–35 | Day 79 | Worksheet 62 | Name |

**?** How did the authors of the Bible know what all God did during the creation, since there was no one to see what He did, how do we know what really happened?

___

**✝** Study and memorize the verse from today (Numbers 23:19), and recite it to your teacher.

**✎** Write out the following passages from your Bible: Malachi 3:6; Luke 21:33; Genesis 1:1.

___

**☺** Draw a picture related to your favorite question of the week and share the meaning with your teacher.

| The Answers Book for Kids Volume 3 | Pages 36–37 | Day 81 | Worksheet 63 | Name |

**?** Where did the Bible come from?

**†** Study and memorize the verse from today (2 Peter 1:21), and recite it to your teacher.

✎ Write out the following passages from your Bible: 2 Timothy 3:16; Psalm 119:89; Proverbs 30:5–6; Matthew 4:4.

Write a short note to a friend about what you studied today.

Elementary Apologetics // 85

| The Answers Book for Kids Volume 3 | Pages 38–39 | Day 82 | Worksheet 64 | Name |

**?** How did God communicate with Moses?

**✝** Study and memorize the verse from today (Exodus 33:11), and recite it to your teacher.

**✎** Write out the following passages from your Bible: Exodus 33:20–23; Exodus 3:4.

**☺** Discuss the answer of today's question with your teacher and why you believe it's important to know.

| The Answers Book for Kids Volume 3 | Pages 40–41 | Day 83 | Worksheet 65 | Name |

**?** Just why is the Bible true? I believe but I just don't understand why it's true.

**✝** Study and memorize the verse from today (2 Timothy 3:16), and recite it to your teacher.

**✎** Write out the following passages from your Bible: 2 Corinthians 5:17; Colossians 1:16–17; John 14:6.

**👥** Write or discuss a question with your teacher that you or a friend has had about God or His world.

Elementary Apologetics

| The Answers Book for Kids Volume 3 | Pages 42–43 | Day 84 | Worksheet 66 | Name |

**?** Why is it that whenever I mention anything about the Bible in school, I get into trouble?

**✝** Study and memorize the verse from today (John 17:14), and recite it to your teacher.

**✎** Write out the following passages from your Bible: Matthew 12:30; James 4:4; Romans 8:7.

**☺** Draw a picture related to your favorite question of the week and share the meaning with your teacher.

88 // Elementary Apologetics

| The Answers Book for Kids Volume 3 | Pages 44–45 | Day 86 | Worksheet 67 | Name |

**?** Why don't we see miracles like they used to in the Bible?

**✝** Study and memorize the verse from today (1 Corinthians 10:11), and recite it to your teacher.

**✏** Write out the following passages from your Bible: Exodus 7:5; John 11:42; 1 Corinthians 15:3–4.

**☺** Write a short note to a friend about what you studied today.

Elementary Apologetics // 89

| | *The Answers Book for Kids Volume 3* | Pages 46–47 | Day 87 | Worksheet 68 | Name |

**?** Why do people believe different things?

✝ Study and memorize the verse from today (Romans 1:18), and recite it to your teacher.

✎ Write out the following passages from your Bible: Genesis 3:6–7; John 5:24.

👥 Discuss the answer of today's question with your teacher and why you believe it's important to know.

Elementary Apologetics

| The Answers Book for Kids Volume 3 | End of Book | Day 89 | Worksheet 69 | Name |

 Match the passage with the biblical book, chapter, and verse from the verses in your book.

Numbers 23:19   John 1:1–3    Romans 5:12    Hebrews 1:1–2   2 Peter 3:8
Jeremiah 23:24  John 17:14    2 Timothy 3:16  2 Peter 1:21   Revelation 1:8

1. _____  God is not a man, that He should lie.

2. _____  "I am the Alpha and the Omega, the Beginning and the End," says the Lord, "who is and who was and who is to come, the Almighty."

3. _____  God, who at various times and in various ways spoke in time past to the fathers by the prophets, has in these last days spoken to us by His Son.

4. _____  ...for prophecy never came by the will of man, but holy men of God spoke as they were moved by the Holy Spirit.

5. _____  Therefore, just as through one man sin entered the world, and death through sin, and thus death spread to all men, because all sinned.

6. _____  "…Do I not fill heaven and earth?" says the LORD.

7. _____  But, beloved, do not forget this one thing, that with the Lord one day is as a thousand years, and a thousand years as one day.

8. _____  All Scripture is given by inspiration of God, and is profitable for doctrine, for reproof, for correction, for instruction in righteousness.

9. _____  In the beginning was the Word, and the Word was with God, and the Word was God. He was in the beginning with God. All things were made through Him.

10. _____  I have given them Your word; and the world has hated them because they are not of the world, just as I am not of the world.

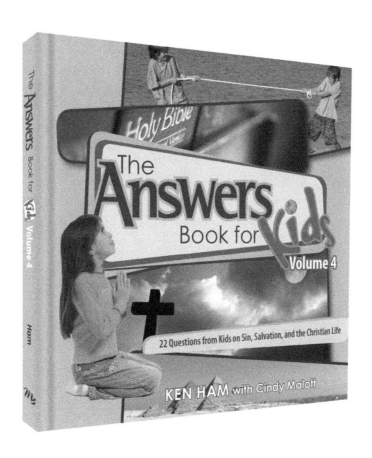

Worksheets

for Use with

*The Answers Book for Kids Volume 4*

| | *The Answers Book for Kids Volume 4* | Pages 4–5 | Day 91 | Worksheet 70 | Name |

**?** Why did God create people when He knew they would sin?

___

___

___

___

___

**✝** Study and memorize the verse from today (Romans 11:33), and recite it to your teacher.

**✎** Write out the following passage from your Bible: Romans 11:36.

___

___

___

___

___

___

___

___

___

___

**☺** Write a short note to a friend about what you studied today.

| | *The Answers Book for Kids Volume 4* | Pages 6–7 | Day 92 | Worksheet 71 | Name |

**?** Could God forgive our sins without the suffering of Christ?

_____

_____

_____

_____

**✝** Study and memorize the verse from today (Acts 4:12), and recite it to your teacher.

**✎** Write out the following passages from your Bible: 2 Corinthians 5:21; Romans 5:8.

_____

_____

_____

_____

_____

_____

_____

_____

**☺** Discuss the answer of today's question with your teacher and why you believe it's important to know.

| The Answers Book for Kids Volume 4 | Pages 8–9 | Day 93 | Worksheet 72 | Name |

**?** Will God and Jesus keep me safe from Satan's fallen angels?

✝ Study and memorize the verses from today (Romans 8:38–39), and recite them to your teacher.

✎ Write out the following passages from your Bible: 1 Peter 5:8; Hebrews 13:5–6.

☺ Write or discuss a question with your teacher that you or a friend has had about God or His world.

Elementary Apologetics // 97

| | The Answers Book for Kids Volume 4 | Pages 10–11 | Day 94 | Worksheet 73 | Name |

**?** When a soldier is in war and he kills someone, is he breaking God's commandments?

_____

_____

_____

_____

**✝** Study and memorize the verse from today (Exodus 20:13), and recite it to your teacher.

**✎** Write out the following passage from your Bible: Genesis 4:6–8.

_____

_____

_____

_____

_____

_____

_____

**☺** Draw a picture related to your favorite question of the week and share the meaning with your teacher.

| The Answers Book for Kids Volume 4 | Pages 12–13 | Day 96 | Worksheet 74 | Name |

**?** When we go to heaven, we have to be perfect up there or wherever. Doesn't that mean our personalities will be changed and everyone will be the same?

**✝** Study and memorize the verse from today (Revelation 21:4), and recite it to your teacher.

**✏** Write out the following passages from your Bible: 1 Corinthians 13:12; 1 John 3:2.

**👥** Write a short note to a friend about what you studied today.

Elementary Apologetics // 99

| The Answers Book for Kids Volume 4 | Pages 14–15 | Day 97 | Worksheet 75 | Name |

**?** Why does God let the bad guys win sometimes?

_____

_____

_____

_____

**†** Study and memorize the verse from today (Habakkuk 1:6), and recite it to your teacher.

**✎** Write out the following passages from your Bible: Psalm 94:1–3; 1 Corinthians 15:24–25.

_____

_____

_____

_____

_____

_____

_____

**☺** Discuss the answer of today's question with your teacher and why you believe it's important to know.

| The Answers Book for Kids Volume 4 | Pages 16–17 | Day 98 | Worksheet 76 | Name |

**?** Why isn't Satan the first sinner instead of Adam and Eve?

**✝** Study and memorize the verse from today (Romans 5:12), and recite it to your teacher.

**✎** Write out the following passages from your Bible: Genesis 1:26; Genesis 2:16–17.

Write or discuss a question with your teacher that you or a friend has had about God or His world.

Elementary Apologetics // 101

| The Answers Book for Kids Volume 4 | Pages 18–19 | Day 99 | Worksheet 77 | Name |

**?** If God is perfect and there was no sin, then where did the sin come from that entered into Lucifer's heart when he became vain?

___

**✝** Study and memorize the verse from today (Colossians 1:16), and recite it to your teacher.

**✎** Write out the following passages from your Bible: Jude 6; Genesis 3:1; John 17:3.

___

**👧** Draw a picture related to your favorite question of the week and share the meaning with your teacher.

| | *The Answers Book for Kids Volume 4* | Pages 20–21 | Day 101 | Worksheet 78 | Name |

**?** Why do animals die? We are the ones who sinned, so why are they punished? They didn't do anything wrong.

___

**✝** Study and memorize the verse from today (Romans 8:22), and recite it to your teacher.

**✎** Write out the following passage from your Bible: Romans 8:20–22.

___

**👥** Write a short note to a friend about what you studied today.

| The Answers Book for Kids Volume 4 | Pages 22–23 | Day 102 | Worksheet 79 | Name |

**?** If I am God's child, then why doesn't He keep me from being sick or hurt here on earth?

**✝** Study and memorize the verse from today (Revelation 21:4), and recite it to your teacher.

**✎** Write out the following passages from your Bible: Genesis 1:31; Genesis 2:17; Genesis 3:6.

**👥** Discuss the answer of today's question with your teacher and why you believe it's important to know.

104 **//** Elementary Apologetics

| The Answers Book for Kids Volume 4 | Pages 24–25 | Day 103 | Worksheet 80 | Name |

**?** If God can control anything, why did He let the tsunami hit and so many people get hurt? Did He create the tsunami?

___

**†** Study and memorize the verse from today (Mark 4:41), and recite it to your teacher.

**✎** Write out the following passage from your Bible: Isaiah 45:7.

___

Write or discuss a question with your teacher that you or a friend has had about God or His world.

*The Answers Book for Kids Volume 4* | Pages 26–27 | Day 104 | Worksheet 81 | Name

**?** Why did Cain kill Abel?

___

**✝** Study and memorize the verse from today (1 John 3:12), and recite it to your teacher.

**✎** Write out the following passage from your Bible: Hebrews 11:4.

___

**☺** Draw a picture related to your favorite question of the week and share the meaning with your teacher.

| The Answers Book for Kids Volume 4 | Pages 28–29 | Day 106 | Worksheet 82 | Name |

**?** What happens to the people who died before Jesus came? Are they in heaven or hell?

**✝** Study and memorize the verses from today (Hebrews 12:22–23), and recite it to your teacher.

**✎** Write out the following passage from your Bible: Hebrews 11:8–10.

**☺** Write a short note to a friend about what you studied today.

Elementary Apologetics // 107

| The Answers Book for Kids Volume 4 | Pages 30–31 | Day 107 | Worksheet 83 | Name |

**Did Adam and Eve go to heaven?**

___

Study and memorize the verse from today (Hebrews 11:4), and recite it to your teacher.

Write out the following passages from your Bible: Genesis 2:18; Genesis 3:8; Genesis 3:21.

___

Discuss the answer of today's question with your teacher and why you believe it's important to know.

| The Answers Book for Kids Volume 4 | Pages 32–33 | Day 108 | Worksheet 84 | Name |

**What is heaven like? Are there really mansions? Will I stay ten forever?**

Study and memorize the verses from today (John 14:2–3), and recite them to your teacher.

Write out the following passages from your Bible: Matthew 6:9; 2 Peter 3:13; 1 Corinthians 15:51–52.

Write or discuss a question with your teacher that you or a friend has had about God or His world.

Elementary Apologetics // 109

| *The Answers Book for Kids Volume 4* | Pages 34–35 | Day 109 | Worksheet 85 | Name |

**?** How will I know what to do when I get to heaven?

_____
_____
_____
_____

**✝** Study and memorize the verse from today (1 Corinthians 2:9), and recite it to your teacher.

**✎** Write out the following passages from your Bible: Revelation 21:4–5; Psalm 16:11.

_____
_____
_____
_____
_____
_____
_____

**☺** Draw a picture related to your favorite question of the week and share the meaning with your teacher.

| The Answers Book for Kids Volume 4 | Pages 36–37 | Day 111 | Worksheet 86 | Name |

**What does being "born again" mean?**

Study and memorize the verse from today (John 3:3), and recite it to your teacher.

Write out the following passages from your Bible: John 1:12; 2 Corinthians 5:17; Romans 10:13.

Write a short note to a friend about what you studied today.

| | The Answers Book for Kids Volume 4 | Pages 38–39 | Day 112 | Worksheet 87 | Name |

**?** When Jesus comes back, why will all of nature (mountains, trees, rocks, etc.) bow down to Him and how will they do that?

_____

_____

_____

_____

✝ Study and memorize the verse from today (Isaiah 55:12), and recite it to your teacher.

✏ Write out the following passages from your Bible: Proverbs 30:5; Psalm 19:8.

_____

_____

_____

_____

_____

_____

👥 Discuss the answer of today's question with your teacher and why you believe it's important to know.

| The Answers Book for Kids Volume 4 | Pages 40–41 | Day 113 | Worksheet 88 | Name |

**?** Why did Jesus preach in the Middle East and not America?

**✝** Study and memorize the verse from today (Matthew 28:19), and recite it to your teacher.

**✏** Write out the following passages from your Bible: Mark 16:15; Acts 1:8.

**☺** Write or discuss a question with your teacher that you or a friend has had about God or His world.

Elementary Apologetics

| The Answers Book for Kids Volume 4 | Pages 42–43 | Day 114 | Worksheet 89 | Name |

**?** Did God cry when Jesus died?

**✝** Study and memorize the verse from today (John 11:35), and recite it to your teacher.

**✏** Write out the following passages from your Bible: John 10:30; John 17:3; Luke 19:41; Isaiah 53:10.

Draw a picture related to your favorite question of the week and share the meaning with your teacher.

| The Answers Book for Kids Volume 4 | Pages 44–45 | Day 116 | Worksheet 90 | Name |

**?** If Satan changed everything by tricking Eve, how do I know Jesus can keep me safe from him?

**✝** Study and memorize the verse from today (1 John 4:4), and recite it to your teacher.

**✎** Write out the following passages from your Bible: Romans 3:23; Romans 6:23; John 3:16; 1 Peter 5:8.

**☺** Write a short note to a friend about what you studied today.

| The Answers Book for Kids Volume 4 | Pages 46–47 | Day 117 | Worksheet 91 | Name |

**?** How do we know other religions aren't true?

_____

_____

_____

_____

**✝** Study and memorize the verse from today (Acts 4:12), and recite it to your teacher.

**✎** Write out the following passages from your Bible: John 10:30; John 14:6; Ephesians 2:8–9.

_____

_____

_____

_____

_____

_____

_____

**☺** Discuss the answer of today's question with your teacher and why you believe it's important to know.

| The Answers Book for Kids Volume 4 | End of Book | Day 119 | Worksheet 92 | Name |

 Match the passage with the biblical book, chapter, and verse from the verses in your book.

Matthew 28:19    John 11:35    Romans 5:12    Romans 11:33    Hebrews 11:4
Mark 4:41        Acts 4:12     Romans 8:22    1 Corinthians 2:9    1 John 4:4

1. _____ But as it is written: "Eye has not seen, nor ear heard, Nor have entered into the heart of man The things which God has prepared for those who love Him."

2. _____ Jesus wept.

3. _____ Go therefore and make disciples of all the nations, baptizing them in the name of the Father and of the Son and of the Holy Spirit.

4. _____ Oh, the depth of the riches both of the wisdom and knowledge of God! How unsearchable are His judgments and His ways past finding out!

5. _____ For we know that the whole creation groans and labors with birth pangs together until now.

6. _____ You are of God, little children, and have overcome them, because He who is in you is greater than he who is in the world.

7. _____ And they feared exceedingly, and said to one another, "Who can this be, that even the wind and the sea obey Him."

8. _____ Nor is there salvation in any other: for there is no other name under heaven given among men by which we must be saved.

9. _____ Therefore, just as through one man sin entered the world, and death through sin, and thus death spread to all men, because all sinned.

10. _____ By faith Abel offered to God a more excellent sacrifice than Cain, through which he obtained witness that he was righteous, God testifying of his gifts; and through it he being dead still speaks.

Elementary Apologetics

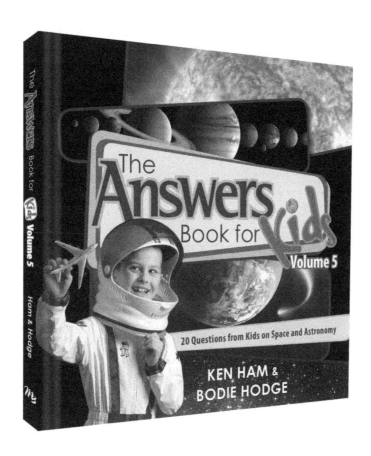

Worksheets

for Use with

*The Answers Book for Kids Volume 5*

| The Answers Book for Kids Volume 5 | Pages 4–5 | Day 121 | Worksheet 93 | Name |

**?** What day were the planets created?

**✝** Study and memorize the verse from today (Genesis 1:17), and recite it to your teacher.

**✏** Write out the following passage from your Bible: Romans 11:36.

**👥** Write a short note to a friend about what you studied today.

Elementary Apologetics

| | *The Answers Book for Kids Volume 5* | Pages 6–7 | Day 122 | Worksheet 94 | Name |

**?** What is the purpose of stars?

**†** Study and memorize the verse from today (Genesis 1:14), and recite it to your teacher.

**✎** Write out the following passages from your Bible: Genesis 1:17; Psalm 136:9; Genesis 15:5; Deuteronomy 10:22; Psalm 19:1.

 Discuss the answer of today's question with your teacher and why you believe it's important to know.

| The Answers Book for Kids Volume 5 | Pages 8–9 | Day 123 | Worksheet 95 | Name |

**?** Where are the "waters" that are "above" the expanse? Is there water at the edge of the universe?

**✝** Study and memorize the verse from today (Genesis 1:7), and recite it to your teacher.

**✏** Write out the following passages from your Bible: Genesis 1:6–8; Genesis 1:17.

**☺** Write or discuss a question with your teacher that you or a friend has had about God or His world.

| The Answers Book for Kids Volume 5 | Pages 10–11 | Day 124 | Worksheet 96 | Name |

**?** Where does a week come from?

**✝** Study and memorize the verse from today (Exodus 20:11), and recite it to your teacher.

**✎** Write out the following passages from your Bible: Exodus 20:11; Exodus 31:17; 1 Timothy 4:7.

**☺** Draw a picture related to your favorite question of the week and share the meaning with your teacher.

|  *The Answers Book for Kids Volume 5* | Pages 12–13 | Day 126 | Worksheet 97 | Name |

**?** What are black holes?

**✝** Study and memorize the verse from today (Colossians 1:16), and recite it to your teacher.

**✏** Write out the following passages from your Bible: Nehemiah 9:6; Revelation 21:1.

**☺** Write a short note to a friend about what you studied today.

Elementary Apologetics  125

| | *The Answers Book for Kids Volume 5* | Pages 14–15 | Day 127 | Worksheet 98 | Name |

**?** Is it possible that there are living things in space?

___

**✝** Study and memorize the verse from today (Isaiah 45:18), and recite it to your teacher.

**✎** Write out the following passages from your Bible: John 4:24; Isaiah 45:18.

___

 Discuss the answer of today's question with your teacher and why you believe it's important to know.

126 **//** Elementary Apologetics

| The Answers Book for Kids Volume 5 | Pages 16–17 | Day 128 | Worksheet 99 | Name |

**?** Is Jupiter stormy?

✝ Study and memorize the verse from today (Psalm 148:8), and recite it to your teacher.

✎ Write out the following passages from your Bible: Job 26:12; Psalm 107:25.

☺ Write or discuss a question with your teacher that you or a friend has had about God or His world.

Elementary Apologetics // 127

| The Answers Book for Kids Volume 5 | Pages 18–19 | Day 129 | Worksheet 100 | Name |

**?** What are comets, and what are they made of?

_____

_____

_____

_____

**✝** Study and memorize the verse from today (Genesis 1:7), and recite it to your teacher.

**✎** Write out the following passage from your Bible: Genesis 5:3–5.

_____

_____

_____

_____

_____

_____

_____

**☺** Draw a picture related to your favorite question of the week and share the meaning with your teacher.

| The Answers Book for Kids Volume 5 | Pages 20–21 | Day 131 | Worksheet 101 | Name |

**?** How far away is the next galaxy?

✝ Study and memorize the verse from today (Isaiah 55:9), and recite it to your teacher.

✏ Write out the following passages from your Bible: Ecclesiastes 3:11; Job 22:12; Psalm 147:4.

 Write a short note to a friend about what you studied today.

| The Answers Book for Kids Volume 5 | Pages 22–23 | Day 132 | Worksheet 102 | Name |

**?** How many planets are there? What is the smallest planet? Could planets hit each other?

___

✝ Study and memorize the verse from today (Job 38:31), and recite it to your teacher.

✎ Write out the following passage from your Bible: Psalm 108:5.

___

Discuss the answer of today's question with your teacher and why you believe it's important to know.

| The Answers Book for Kids Volume 5 | Pages 24–25 | Day 133 | Worksheet 103 | Name |

**?** Did Christians believe the earth was flat?

**✝** Study and memorize the verse from today (Isaiah 40:22), and recite it to your teacher.

**✏** Write out the following passages from your Bible: Isaiah 40:22; Job 26:7; Job 26:10.

**☺** Write or discuss a question with your teacher that you or a friend has had about God or His world.

| The Answers Book for Kids Volume 5 | Pages 26–27 | Day 134 | Worksheet 104 | Name |

**?** Do meteors burn up, and are they dangerous?

___

**✝** Study and memorize the verse from today (Ecclesiastes 7:17), and recite to it your teacher.

**✎** Write out the following passages from your Bible: Ecclesiastes 3:1; Romans 8:22.

___

**☺** Draw a picture related to your favorite question of the week and share the meaning with your teacher.

132 // Elementary Apologetics

| The Answers Book for Kids Volume 5 | Pages 28–29 | Day 136 | Worksheet 105 | Name |

**?** How hot are the sun and other stars?

**✝** Study and memorize the verse from today (James 1:11), and recite it to your teacher.

**✏** Write out the following passage from your Bible: 1 Corinthians 15:41.

**☺** Write a short note to a friend about what you studied today.

| | *The Answers Book for Kids Volume 5* | Pages 30–31 | Day 137 | Worksheet 106 | Name |

**?** What is the farthest that we've sent something into space?

**✝** Study and memorize the verse from today (Mark 13:27), and recite it to your teacher.

**✎** Write out the following passages from your Bible: Isaiah 55:9; Ephesians 4:10; Luke 19:10.

 Discuss the answer of today's question with your teacher and why you believe it's important to know.

| The Answers Book for Kids Volume 5 | Pages 32–33 | Day 138 | Worksheet 107 | Name |

**?** What are the rings of planets made from?

**†** Study and memorize the verse from today (Psalm 31:3), and recite it to your teacher.

**✎** Write out the following passage from your Bible: Colossians 1:15–17.

**☺** Write or discuss a question with your teacher that you or a friend has had about God or His world.

Elementary Apologetics // 135

| The Answers Book for Kids Volume 5 | Pages 34–35 | Day 139 | Worksheet 108 | Name |

**What about the big bang?**

Study and memorize the verse from today (Nehemiah 9:6), and recite it to your teacher.

Write out the following passages from your Bible: Isaiah 44:24; Zechariah 12:1.

Draw a picture related to your favorite question of the week and share the meaning with your teacher.

| The Answers Book for Kids Volume 5 | Pages 36–37 | Day 141 | Worksheet 109 | Name |

**?** How big is our galaxy?

**†** Study and memorize the verse from today (1 Kings 8:27), and recite it to your teacher.

**✎** Write out the following passages from your Bible: Job 9:9; Job 38:31; Amos 5:8.

**☺** Write a short note to a friend about what you studied today.

| | The Answers Book for Kids Volume 5 | Pages 38–39 | Day 142 | Worksheet 110 | Name |

**?** Will the sun ever run out or blow up?

**✝** Study and memorize the verse from today (Psalms 72:5), and recite it to your teacher.

**✎** Write out the following passages from your Bible: Genesis 1:31; Genesis 8:22; Romans 8:22; 2 Peter 3:13.

 Discuss the answer of today's question with your teacher and why you believe it's important to know.

| The Answers Book for Kids Volume 5 | Pages 40–41 | Day 143 | Worksheet 111 | Name |

**?** What would happen if a comet ran into an asteroid?

_____

_____

_____

_____

✝ Study and memorize the verse from today (Romans 1:20), and recite it to your teacher.

✎ Write out the following passage from your Bible: Genesis 1:14.

_____

_____

_____

_____

_____

_____

_____

_____

 Write or discuss a question with your teacher that you or a friend has had about God or His world.

| *The Answers Book for Kids Volume 5* | Pages 42–43 | Day 144 | Worksheet 112 | Name |

**?** How old is space and the universe?

___

**✝** Study and memorize the verse from today (Genesis 1:1), and recite it to your teacher.

**✎** Write out the following passages from your Bible: Genesis 1:1; Isaiah 42:5; Hebrews 11:3.

___

**☺** Draw a picture related to your favorite question of the week and share the meaning with your teacher.

| The Answers Book for Kids Volume 5 | Pages 44–45 | Day 146 | Worksheet 113 | Name |

 Solve this word search with the list of planets, dwarf planets, and other words from this book.

| O | E | S | A | R | Y | R | U | C | R | E | M | R | E |
|---|---|---|---|---|---|---|---|---|---|---|---|---|---|
| U | U | J | U | P | I | T | E | R | P | A | N | E | R |
| H | R | N | U | M | C | E | Y | X | A | L | A | G | E |
| M | E | A | I | T | E | A | S | T | E | R | O | I | D |
| S | K | N | N | V | R | T | E | N | U | T | P | E | N |
| M | A | S | U | U | E | R | E | H | A | U | M | E | A |
| O | M | T | H | R | S | R | U | O | P | A | E | M | O |
| O | E | R | U | S | S | V | S | N | R | U | V | T | A |
| N | K | E | U | R | V | E | M | E | T | S | U | H | E |
| S | A | N | S | R | N | N | C | U | E | L | P | T | S |
| R | M | I | R | A | R | U | A | O | P | T | K | R | K |
| S | R | M | R | T | L | S | E | E | M | S | R | A | M |
| E | L | H | N | S | R | A | T | S | T | E | K | E | O |
| S | E | L | O | H | K | C | A | L | B | I | T | E | R |

Asteroid    Eris       Mars       Neptune    Sun
Black Holes Galaxy     Mercury    Pluto      Universe
Ceres       Haumea     Meteors    Saturn     Uranus
Comet       Jupiter    Moon       Stars      Venus
Earth       Makemake

**The Answers Book for Kids Volume 5** | Pages 46–47 | Day 147 | Worksheet 114 | Name

Fill in the crossword puzzle with the correct words from the terms on pages 46–47.

**Across:**

4. Rocky fragments even smaller than asteroids, found in many parts of space.
5. These are among the most distant and brightest (luminous) objects we know of.
7. A measure of how far light can travel in one year, roughly 5,878,625,000,000 miles or 9,460,730,000,000 km.
9. These are massive enough to be nearly round, in orbit around the sun (usually in the same basic plane), and have control of its surroundings (e.g., moons, rings, and so on revolve around it).

**Down:**

1. Large cloud-like structures (interstellar) made of dust and gases that give off light in beautiful arrays and shapes.
2. These do not fulfill all the requirements of a planet but are significantly larger than asteroids.
3. Rocky bodies too small to be planets, usually with an irregular shape.
6. Systems of billions of stars held together by gravity.
8. Object made mostly of ice, frozen gas, dust, and rock that makes long elliptical orbits around the sun.

142 // Elementary Apologetics

| The Answers Book for Kids Volume 5 | End of Book | Day 149 | Worksheet 115 | Name |

Match the passage with the biblical book, chapter, and verse from the verses in your book.

Genesis 1:1    Exodus 20:11    Psalm 31:3    Ecclesiastes 7:17    Romans 1:20
Genesis 1:7    Job 38:31       Psalm 72:5    Isaiah 55:9          Colossians 1:16

1. _____  Do not be overly wicked, Nor be foolish: Why should you die before your time?

2. _____  For since the creation of the world His invisible attributes are clearly seen, being understood by the things that are made, even His eternal power and Godhead, so that they are without excuse.

3. _____  Thus God made the firmament, and divided the waters which were under the firmament from the waters which were above the firmament; and it was so.

4. _____  Can you bind the cluster of the Pleiades, Or loose the belt of Orion?

5. _____  For as the heavens are higher than the earth, So are My ways higher than your ways, and My thoughts than your thoughts.

6. _____  For You are my rock and my fortress; Therefore, for Your name's sake, Lead me and guide me.

7. _____  In the beginning God created the heavens and the earth.

8. _____  For in six days the LORD made the heavens and the earth, the sea, and all that is in them, and rested the seventh day. Therefore the LORD blessed the Sabbath day and hallowed it.

9. _____  For by Him all things were created that are in heaven and that are on earth, visible and invisible, whether thrones or dominions or principalities or powers. All things were created through Him and for Him.

10. _____  They shall fear You As long as the sun and moon endure, Throughout all generations.

Elementary Apologetics

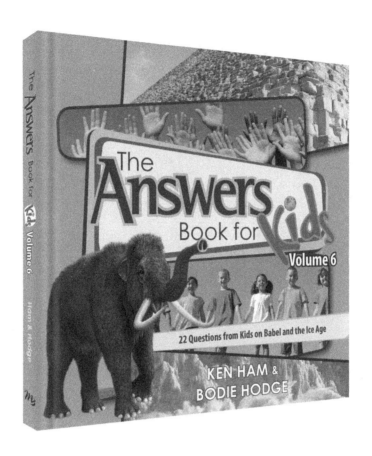

Worksheets

for Use with

*The Answers Book for Kids Volume 6*

| The Answers Book for Kids Volume 6 | Pages 4–5 | Day 151 | Worksheet 116 | Name |

**?** Where was the Tower of Babel built?

**✝** Study and memorize the verse from today (Genesis 11:2), and recite it to your teacher.

**✎** Write out the following passages from your Bible: 2 Kings 20:14; Daniel 11:1.

**☺** Write a short note to a friend about what you studied today.

| | *The Answers Book for Kids Volume 6* | Pages 6–7 | Day 152 | Worksheet 117 | Name |

**?** How big was the Tower of Babel?

**✝** Study and memorize the verse from today (Genesis 11:4), and recite it to your teacher.

**✎** Write out the following passages from your Bible: Genesis 11:3–4; Proverbs 18:10.

**☺** Discuss the answer of today's question with your teacher and why you believe it's important to know.

| The Answers Book for Kids Volume 6 | Pages 8–9 | Day 153 | Worksheet 118 | Name |

**?** How long did it take to build the Tower of Babel?

**✝** Study and memorize the verse from today (Genesis 11:3), and recite it to your teacher.

**✎** Write out the following passage from your Bible: Genesis 11:5–6.

**☺** Write or discuss a question with your teacher that you or a friend has had about God or His world.

| The Answers Book for Kids Volume 6 | Pages 10–11 | Day 154 | Worksheet 119 | Name |

**?** How many people did it take to build the Tower?

___

**†** Study and memorize the verse from today (Genesis 10:32), and recite it to your teacher.

**✎** Write out the following passages from your Bible: Genesis 9:1; Genesis 11:4.

___

 Draw a picture related to your favorite question of the week and share the meaning with your teacher.

| The Answers Book for Kids Volume 6 | Pages 12–13 | Day 156 | Worksheet 120 | Name |

**?** What time period was the Tower of Babel built in?

___

**†** Study and memorize the verse from today (Genesis 10:1), and recite it to your teacher.

**✎** Write out the following passages from your Bible: Genesis 10:32; Genesis 12:10; Galatians 3:28.

___

**☺** Write a short note to a friend about what you studied today.

| The Answers Book for Kids Volume 6 | Pages 14–15 | Day 157 | Worksheet 121 | Name |

**?** Is the Tower of Babel still here?

**✝** Study and memorize the verse from today (Genesis 11:8), and recite it to your teacher.

**✎** Write out the following passages from your Bible: Job 3:14; Daniel 4:27.

 Discuss the answer of today's question with your teacher and why you believe it's important to know.

| The Answers Book for Kids Volume 6 | Pages 16–17 | Day 158 | Worksheet 122 | Name |

**?** Are there any archaeological remains of the Tower of Babel?

**✝** Study and memorize the verse from today (Job 3:14), and recite it to your teacher.

**✎** Write out the following passage from your Bible: 2 Kings 19:25.

**☺** Write or discuss a question with your teacher that you or a friend has had about God or His world.

Elementary Apologetics // 153

**?** Was there anything inside the Tower of Babel?

✝ Study and memorize the verse from today (Genesis 11:4), and recite it to your teacher.

✏ Write out the following passages from your Bible: Job 15:28; Judges 9:52; Acts 7:49.

 Draw a picture related to your favorite question of the week and share the meaning with your teacher.

| The Answers Book for Kids Volume 6 | Pages 20–21 | Day 161 | Worksheet 124 | Name |

**?** Why was Babel made?

___

**✝** Study and memorize the verse from today (Genesis 11:4), and recite it to your teacher.

**✏** Write out the following passages from your Bible: Genesis 9:1; Genesis 11:4.

___

**☺** Write a short note to a friend about what you studied today.

Elementary Apologetics 155

| The Answers Book for Kids Volume 6 | Pages 22–23 | Day 162 | Worksheet 125 | Name |

**?** If everyone would have scattered like God said, would there still be one language?

**✝** Study and memorize the verse from today (Genesis 11:9), and recite it to your teacher.

**✎** Write out the following passage from your Bible: Acts 2:4–6.

 Discuss the answer of today's question with your teacher and why you believe it's important to know.

| The Answers Book for Kids Volume 6 | Pages 24–25 | Day 163 | Worksheet 126 | Name |

**?** How many languages came from Babel?

___

**✝** Study and memorize the verse from today (Genesis 11:6), and recite it to your teacher.

**✏** Write out the following passages from your Bible: Genesis 10:32; Genesis 11:13–14.

___

**☺** Write or discuss a question with your teacher that you or a friend has had about God or His world.

| The Answers Book for Kids Volume 6 | Pages 26–27 | Day 164 | Worksheet 127 | Name |

**?** How did people with different skin color get on the earth?

**✝** Study and memorize the verse from today (Jeremiah 13:23), and recite it to your teacher.

**✏** Write out the following passages from your Bible: Genesis 11:9; Acts 17:26; John 3:16.

**☺** Draw a picture related to your favorite question of the week and share the meaning with your teacher.

| The Answers Book for Kids Volume 6 | Pages 28–29 | Day 166 | Worksheet 128 | Name |

**?** When people spread out, how did they make it to America?

✝ Study and memorize the verse from today (Genesis 11:9), and recite it to your teacher.

✎ Write out the following passages from your Bible: Genesis 6:14; Genesis 6:22; Genesis 10:5.

 Write a short note to a friend about what you studied today.

| | *The Answers Book for Kids Volume 6* | Pages 30–31 | Day 167 | Worksheet 129 | Name |

**?** Where did the Chinese people come from?

**✝** Study and memorize the verse from today (Isaiah 49:12), and recite it to your teacher.

**✎** Write out the following passages from your Bible: Genesis 10:15–17; Isaiah 49:12.

 Discuss the answer of today's question with your teacher and why you believe it's important to know.

| The Answers Book for Kids Volume 6 | Pages 32–33 | Day 168 | Worksheet 130 | Name |

**?** Where do the English people come from?

**†** Study and memorize the verse from today (Genesis 10:3), and recite it to your teacher.

**✎** Write out the following passage from your Bible: Jeremiah 51:27.

**☺** Write or discuss a question with your teacher that you or a friend has had about God or His world.

Elementary Apologetics

| *The Answers Book for Kids Volume 6* | Pages 34–35 | Day 169 | Worksheet 131 | Name |

**?** Where did the Japanese and other peoples come from?

___

___

___

___

**✝** Study and memorize the verse from today (Genesis 10:4), and recite it to your teacher.

**✎** Write out the following passage from your Bible: Genesis 10:4–5.

___

___

___

___

___

___

___

**👥** Draw a picture related to your favorite question of the week and share the meaning with your teacher.

162 // Elementary Apologetics

| The Answers Book for Kids Volume 6 | Pages 36–37 | Day 171 | Worksheet 132 | Name |

**?** What is the Ice Age?

_____

_____

_____

_____

**✝** Study and memorize the verse from today (Job 6:16), and recite it to your teacher.

**✎** Write out the following passages from your Bible: Job 6:16–17; Job 38:22–23.

_____

_____

_____

_____

_____

_____

_____

_____

**☺** Write a short note to a friend about what you studied today.

Elementary Apologetics

| *The Answers Book for Kids Volume 6* | Pages 38–39 | Day 172 | Worksheet 133 | Name |

**How does an Ice Age happen?**

Study and memorize the verse from today (Job 38:29), and recite it to your teacher.

Write out the following passages from your Bible: Genesis 7:11; Psalm 104:8–9.

Discuss the answer of today's question with your teacher and why you believe it's important to know.

| The Answers Book for Kids Volume 6 | Pages 40–41 | Day 173 | Worksheet 134 | Name |

**?** What was the extent of the Ice Age?

**†** Study and memorize the verse from today (Job 37:10), and recite it to your teacher.

**✎** Write out the following passages from your Bible: Job 6:16; Job 24:19; Job 38:22.

**☺** Write or discuss a question with your teacher that you or a friend has had about God or His world.

| | *The Answers Book for Kids Volume 6* | Pages 42–43 | Day 174 | Worksheet 135 | Name |

**?** Has anyone ever found a frozen person from the Ice Age?

**✞** Study and memorize the verse from today (Luke 21:18), and recite it to your teacher.

**✎** Write out the following passages from your Bible: Hebrews 9:27; Ephesians 2:8.

**☺** Draw a picture related to your favorite question of the week and share the meaning with your teacher.

| The Answers Book for Kids Volume 6 | Pages 44–45 | Day 176 | Worksheet 136 | Name |

**?** How did animals make it to America and Australia after the Flood?

**✝** Study and memorize the verse from today (Genesis 8:17), and recite it to your teacher.

**✏** Write out the following passages from your Bible: Genesis 9:28; Genesis 11:10–11; Genesis 10:5.

**☺** Write a short note to a friend about what you studied today.

| The Answers Book for Kids Volume 6 | Pages 46–47 | Day 177 | Worksheet 137 | Name |

**?** What kinds of animals lived in the areas affected by the Ice Age?

___

✝ Study and memorize the verse from today (Proverbs 12:10), and recite it to your teacher.

✏ Write out the following passages from your Bible: Genesis 1:29; Genesis 9:3; Mark 7:19.

___

☺ Discuss the answer of today's question with your teacher and why you believe it's important to know.

| | | | | |
|---|---|---|---|---|
| The Answers Book for Kids Volume 6 | End of Book | Day 179 | Worksheet 138 | Name |

Match the passage with the biblical book, chapter, and verse from the verses in your book.

Genesis 10:32   Genesis 11:8   Job 6:16   Job 38:29   Isaiah 49:12
Genesis 11:4   Genesis 11:9   Job 37:10   Proverbs 12:10   Luke 21:18

1. _____  And they said, "Come, let us build ourselves a city, and a tower whose top is in the heavens; let us make a name for ourselves, lest we be scattered abroad over the face of the whole earth."

2. _____  "But not a hair of your head shall be lost."

3. _____  A righteous man regards the life of his animal, But the tender mercies of the wicked are cruel.

4. _____  From whose womb comes the ice? And the frost of heaven, who gives it birth?

5. _____  "Surely these shall come from afar; Look! Those from the north and the west, and these from the land of Sinim."

6. _____  Therefore its name is called Babel, because there the LORD confused the language of all the earth; and from there the LORD scattered them abroad over the face of all the earth.

7. _____  Which are dark because of the ice, And into which the snow vanishes.

8. _____  These were the families of the sons of Noah, according to their generations, in their nations; and from these the nations were divided on the earth after the flood.

9. _____  So the LORD scattered them abroad from there over the face of all the earth, and they ceased building the city.

10. _____  By the breath of God ice is given, And the broad waters are frozen.

Elementary Apologetics

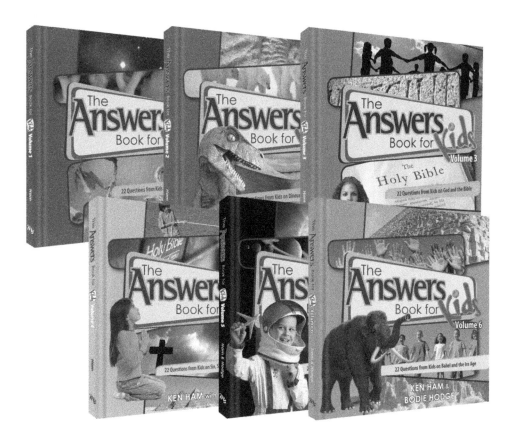

# Quizzes

## for Use with

## *The Answers Book for Kids Volumes 1–6*

**The Answers Book for Kids Volume 1** | End of Book | Day 28 | Quiz 1 | Name

Fill in the blank with the missing word from the word bank.

| 24 | control | evolution | pattern | power |
| characteristics | different | obey | planets | proud |

1. God created everything by His great _____.

2. God make a week seven days long to set a _____ for us to follow.

3. God let Adam name the animals to help him see that he was completely _____ than the animals.

4. Adam named only land animals on the sixth day, so it would have taken under _____ hours.

5. God put the tree in the Garden of Eden to test and see if Adam really did love God enough to totally _____ Him.

6. Lucifer was one of the beautiful angels God had created, but he soon became _____ and wanted to take God's place on His throne.

7. The _____ were created on the fourth day.

8. _____ is a word that means "change."

9. Evolutionists don't want to admit that God is in _____ of all things.

10. God created all living things, and it makes sense that a lot of these share many similar _____.

Elementary Apologetics

**The Answers Book for Kids Volume 2** | End of Book | Day 58 | Quiz 2 | Name

Fill in the blank with the missing word from the word bank.

| death | dinosaurs | people | rose | search |
| decayed | melanin | petroglyphs | sea | warm |

1. All the kinds of land animals were on the ark, including _____.

2. The Bible doesn't mention _____ animals on the ark.

3. Meat-eating animals came about because of sin, violence, and _____ in the world.

4. Once Noah and his family got off the ark, it may have provided building materials for their homes, it may have _____, been used as firewood, or been destroyed by other means.

5. Noah did not have to _____ the world for the animals because God commanded them to come to the ark.

6. The Bible says that the mountains _____ and the Flood waters went down where the ocean basins formed.

7. There are drawings that people carved long ago on rocks, and some of these _____ look a lot like dinosaurs.

8. When you do the calculations, you will find that it is very easy to account for six billion _____ starting with only eight after the Flood.

9. As the _____ water from the oceans evaporated into the air, forming clouds, the colder air over the earth caused wintry conditions, lots of snow, and ice glaciers.

10. We all have the same type of skin color, but it is just that the amount of _____ differs from person to person.

Elementary Apologetics // 175

| | The Answers Book for Kids Volume 3 | End of Book | Day 88 | Quiz 3 | Name |
|---|---|---|---|---|---|

Fill in the blank with the missing word from the word bank.

| created | infinite | Jesus | Moses | sinned |
| glory | inspired | judged | schools | sinners |

1. What does God look like? Though we cannot see God, we see the _____ of God in the face of Jesus Christ as revealed in the Bible.

2. When we talk about how big God is, we need to understand that God is _____.

3. When Adam and Eve sinned (disobeyed God) in the Garden, the Bible tells us that in Adam the whole human race _____ and fell.

4. God _____ the sin in the world by punishing His Son on the cross.

5. God _____ us to glorify Him and to enjoy Him forever.

6. The Bible came from holy men of God who were _____ by God through the Holy Spirit working in their hearts.

7. The Bible tells us that God spoke out loud to _____ many times as he led the Israelites to the Promised Land.

8. We can rely on the Bible's truth concerning _____ — for instance, in considering how many prophecies about Him were made hundreds of years before He came to earth as a man.

9. When we try to keep God out of _____, we end up teaching the kids that there is no God.

10. People believe so many different things because they are _____ and they don't want to listen to God.

Elementary Apologetics

**The Answers Book for Kids Volume 4** | End of Book | Day 118 | Quiz 4 | Name

 Mark each statement with either a "T" for true or an "F" for false.

_____ 1. God could forgive our sins without the suffering of Christ because we can choose to do good things instead of bad.

_____ 2. The Bible says that all things will die on earth because of Adam's sin in the Garden of Eden.

_____ 3. The people who loved God and who died before Christ were saved by faith.

_____ 4. The Bible states that Adam and Eve went to heaven when they died.

_____ 5. Being born again means becoming part of God's family — the word "again" literally means "from above."

_____ 6. When God tells us that the mountains and the hills will cry out and the trees will clap their hands, this is meant to be taken literally.

_____ 7. Jesus preached in the Middle East because this is where He felt most at home.

_____ 8. God wanted to show us how much He loved us by sending His only Son to earth.

_____ 9. Any religion that claims to be true MUST believe that Jesus is God.

_____ 10. The Bible tells us that one day we will have new physical bodies that will be different from the bodies we have now.

| The Answers Book for Kids Volume 5 | End of Book | Day 148 | Quiz 5 | Name |

 Mark each statement with either a "T" for true or an "F" for false.

_____ 1. God created stars to give light, for comparison, and to declare the glory of God.

_____ 2. The Bible seems clear that there is intelligent life in outer space.

_____ 3. Comets are icy objects in space that release dust or gas when they approach the sun.

_____ 4. The Bible teaches against a flat earth in Isaiah 40:22 and Job 26:10.

_____ 5. If some parts of a comet don't burn up, those pieces are called "meteorites."

_____ 6. We have sent something that has finally reached the outer edges of our solar system and is about to enter interstellar space, which is called the *Voyager 1* spacecraft.

_____ 7. The rings of the planets are made up of dust, rock, and ice.

_____ 8. The big bang basically teaches that the universe created itself.

_____ 9. Our galaxy is called the Milky Way and is about 112,000 light-years across.

_____ 10. The universe is around 6,000 years old.

Elementary Apologetics

| The Answers Book for Kids Volume 6 | End of Book | Day 178 | Quiz 6 | Name |

Fill in the blank with the missing word from the word bank.

7 to 8         100        4,200      Flood      melanin
78             350        English    Job        Ötzi

1. The Tower of Babel was probably about _____ stories and 300 feet high.

2. The Bible in Genesis 10 gives a list of at least _____ families that came out of Babel with new languages.

3. The Tower of Babel incident occurred around _____ years ago — about 100 years after the Flood.

4. If you tally the existing language families up around the world, there are less than _____ today.

5. We all have the same basic skin color, from the main pigment in our skin called "_____."

6. "Angles" is where we get the name _____ from (think "Anglish").

7. The Ice Age was an event that happened after the _____ because the oceans would have been warmer and the land cooler.

8. It is possible that _____, who lived in the Middle East near the Jordan River, even saw some snow and ice that could have been associated with the time of the Ice Age.

9. They have found a man frozen in a glacier and named him "_____, the Iceman."

10. During the Ice Age, most think that the ocean level dropped by about _____ feet.

Elementary Apologetics // 183

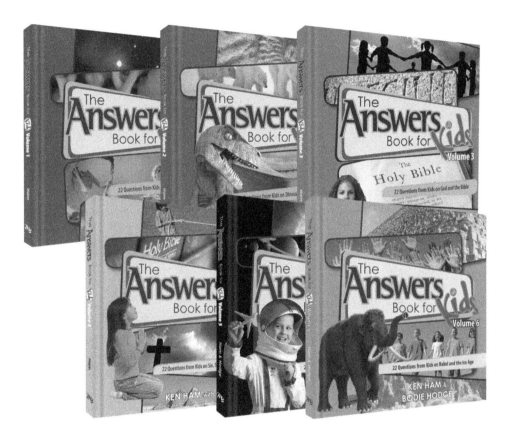

# Answers for Worksheets and Quizzes for Use with

## *The Answers Book for Kids Volumes 1–6*

# Answers Book for Kids Volume 1 — Worksheet Answer Keys

**Worksheet 1**

Time began when God started to create everything in the whole universe. He did this "in the beginning" of the Creation Week. According to the Bible, that was about 6,000 years ago.

**Worksheet 2**

God created by His great power. God needed only to speak and everything was created.

**Worksheet 3**

Bellybuttons are scars left over from when we were born. The Bible tells us that our great God made the first man (Adam) directly out of dust. He was already an adult, so he didn't need a cord to get food. The Bible also tells us that God made the first woman (Eve) directly from the rib of the man. So, she was an adult, too.

**Worksheet 4**

We just have no idea. The worldwide flood of Noah's day would have destroyed everything on the earth, including the Garden of Eden.

**Worksheet 5**

Yes, the first two verses of Genesis 1 describe events on the very same day.

**Worksheet 6**

It seems that God created the trees to sprout, grow, and bear fruit all in one day. Trees most likely had growth rings for a couple of reasons. First, they were fully grown trees to start with, and most grown trees have growth rings. Second, the growth rings of many trees are actually part of the structure of the tree and support the tree.

**Worksheet 7**

God was setting a pattern for us to follow. If we just kept on working every single day, we would get very tired and probably get sick. God was showing us that we can work six days, but then we need to rest for one day.

**Worksheet 8**

Adam was the leader of that very first family. Adam was not better or more valuable than Eve. It was just that God knew someone had to be the leader, so He made that leader Adam. By doing this, God showed us that He wants the husband, the dad in the family, to be the spiritual leader in the family.

**Worksheet 9**

God was teaching Adam and us a lesson. As Adam was naming the animals, it became very clear to him that he was completely different from the animals and was a special creation.

**Worksheet 10**

He would have only named the "kinds" of animals that God brought to him. We don't know what language Adam spoke, so there is really no way of knowing what he called each animal kind.

**Worksheet 11**

Adam named only land animals on the sixth day. This means that he definitely named them within 24 hours.

**Worksheet 12**

Whenever it will serve God's perfect plan, He can use anything to convey His message, even a donkey. In the same way, God allowed Satan (the devil) to use the serpent to disguise himself and tempt Eve.

**Worksheet 13**

When God made Adam, He didn't want him to be a puppet, but He wanted Adam to truly love Him. The command about the tree of the knowledge of good and evil was God's test to see if Adam really did love God enough to totally obey Him.

**Worksheet 14**

Lucifer (or Satan) was very good when God created him. In fact, Lucifer was one of the beautiful angels God had created! But he soon became proud and wanted to take God's place on His throne.

**Worksheet 15**

Most people believe that Cain married his sister or his niece, and the Bible does not tell us what her name was. Way back then (about 6,000 years ago), close relatives could marry — they had to in order to start their own families.

### Worksheet 16
It is likely that the bumblebees had what we now call stingers before sin, but they weren't used to harm anything.

### Worksheet 17
They may have been in the Garden only a few days before they sinned and God made them leave.

### Worksheet 18
Our Bible verse tells us that God made the sun, moon, and stars on the fourth day.

### Worksheet 19
When we hear the term light-year, we need to realize it is not a measure of time but a measure of distance, telling us how far away something is.

### Worksheet 20
The word evolution actually just means "change." When most people hear the word evolution today, they think of Charles Darwin. Darwin believed that one kind of animal evolved into a totally different kind and that eventually ape-like creatures evolved into human beings over millions of years.

### Worksheet 21
We are all born sinners, and because of that, people just don't want to admit that a powerful, all-knowing God created them. They don't want to admit that God is in control of all things.

### Worksheet 22
God created all living things, and it makes sense that a lot of these share many similar characteristics or design. The same God, the same Designer, created both monkeys and humans, and thus there are some similarities. But the differences are also important.

### Worksheet 23
1. Exodus 20:11
2. Genesis 1:21
3. Psalm 19:1
4. Genesis 1:31
5. Genesis 1:1
6. Romans 8:22
7. Genesis 1:5
8. Genesis 2:17
9. Genesis 1:26
10. Genesis 2:18

## Answers Book for Kids Volume 2 — Worksheet Answer Keys

### Worksheet 24
The people were probably a bit different back before the Flood because they spoke the same language and looked more similar than humans do today — but we are still humans belonging to one race.

### Worksheet 25
All the kinds of land animals were on the ark. Well, that just had to include the dinosaur kinds, too!

### Worksheet 26
There were probably only about 50 actual kinds, and the average size of a dinosaur is the size of a sheep.

### Worksheet 27
The Bible doesn't mention sea animals on the ark.

### Worksheet 28
God said to take food on board. It could be that God told Noah exactly what to take, but it just wasn't written down.

### Worksheet 29
God could have miraculously stopped animals from eating each other. God could also have supernaturally caused the animals to hibernate much of the time. And Noah no doubt built cages or rooms with doors to keep the animals from roaming the ark and possibly hurting other animals.

### Worksheet 30
Because of sin, violence and death came into the world. Now, many animals eat other animals. But the Bible tells us that one day Jesus will restore His creation to its perfect state. There will no longer be sickness or death, and animals won't eat each other.

## Worksheet 31

Sin changed everything. With it came death, sickness, and suffering. Changes occurred in the weather, the food supply, the behavior of people, and the behavior of animals. These (and other) changes have contributed to why many animals have gone extinct.

## Worksheet 32

The ark may have provided building materials for the homes and other buildings they would all eventually need. It may have decayed, been used as firewood, or been destroyed by other means.

## Worksheet 33

The Flood was cataclysmic — it was dreadful, tragic, disastrous, devastating. It destroyed everything and everyone on earth, just as it was intended to do.

## Worksheet 34

We don't know for sure, but it seems that we should at least allow the possibility that some could have been tamed to help with transportation, maybe even farming, hauling heavy loads (the strong ones!), and other things.

## Worksheet 35

Noah did not have to search the world for the animals because God commanded them to come to the ark.

## Worksheet 36

The Bible says that the mountains rose up and the Flood waters went down where the ocean basins formed.

## Worksheet 37

It is probable that as the Flood rose, humans continued to seek higher ground. However, there may be some human fossils somewhere in the world.

## Worksheet 38

We do have something called petroglyphs. These are drawings that people carved long ago on rocks. Some of these petroglyphs look a lot like dinosaurs.

## Worksheet 39

They simply died. After the Flood, and to this very day, there are many animals that have become extinct or are on the endangered species list because of the effects of sin on the earth.

## Worksheet 40

Dinosaurs lived with people — before the Flood, on Noah's ark with Noah and his family, and after the Flood. God's Word also describes a dinosaur in the book of Job.

## Worksheet 41

Dinosaurs were made on Day 6. So, actually, dinosaurs were created after birds and could never have turned into birds! Also, birds and dinosaurs have different systems of breathing, they have completely different blood systems, and they have very different bone structures.

## Worksheet 42

When you do the calculations, you will find that it is very easy to account for six billion people starting with only eight after the Flood.

## Worksheet 43

When the Flood ended, the mountains rose, the valleys sank, and the water flowed off the earth's surface and seeped through the soft sediments. Because water can contain acid dissolved from the air and the soil, this would eat away at the limestone forming caves.

## Worksheet 44

The Bible tells us that the fountains of the great deep burst forth. This breaking up of the earth caused the oceans to heat up and caused ash and dust to fill the air, blocking out sunlight, making the temperatures on earth cooler. As the warm water from the oceans evaporated into the air, forming clouds, the colder air over the earth caused wintry conditions, lots of snow, and ice glaciers.

## Worksheet 45

We all do have the same type of skin color. It is just that the amount of melanin (brown color) differs from person to person.

## Worksheet 46

1. Genesis 11:1, 7
2. Job 40:15
3. Genesis 6:19

4. Job 30:6
5. Genesis 1:20, 23
6. Genesis 6:7
7. Psalm 104:8 ESV
8. Genesis 6:21
9. Genesis 8:1
10. Genesis 9:1

# Answers Book for Kids Volume 3 — Worksheet Answer Keys

**Worksheet 47**

God—the God of the Bible—is the Creator of everything. Nothing and no one is bigger than Him. He was not created but has always existed.

**Worksheet 48**

While we are here on earth, we cannot see Him, we cannot know what He looks like, even though He is present with us. However, we see the glory of God in the face of Jesus Christ as revealed in the Bible.

**Worksheet 49**

We can't see God because He is a spirit. The Bible tells us He is omnipresent by His Spirit. That means He is everywhere and sees everything all the time.

**Worksheet 50**

When we talk about how big God is, we need to understand that God is infinite. (Infinite means we can't even measure it and there are no words to describe it — it is forever big.)

**Worksheet 51**

Although we can't completely understand His power, we know He is infinite in power (meaning there is no way to measure it), and all power ultimately comes from Him and the source of His power never becomes exhausted.

**Worksheet 52**

The Bible tells us about times when God was sad (during Noah's day) and when God is happy (when we obey His Word). So, yes, God can laugh with joy.

**Worksheet 53**

God is outside of time — to Him a day is like a thousand years, and a thousand years are like a day. He, therefore, knows everything before it happens. He even created time. He is not bound by time, and He sees all of life and history from start to finish at the same time!

**Worksheet 54**

God is three distinct persons — Father, Son, and Holy Spirit — and each is fully God, yet there is only one God. This is especially hard for us to understand. But, remember, God is not like anything else in the whole world.

**Worksheet 55**

Yes, the Holy Spirit is even (equal) with God because the Holy Spirit IS God.

**Worksheet 56**

God promises that if we study His Word we will get to know Him. We need to read it and study it. We need to trust it. When we do that, we WILL hear God through His Word!

**Worksheet 57**

There are no coincidences with God because He always works all things together according to His plan. He is in charge of everything, and His plans always work out.

**Worksheet 58**

God did NOT create sin. When God created people, He knew we would disobey Him — though He created Adam and Eve with the potential to sin. And when Adam and Eve sinned (disobeyed God) in the Garden, the Bible tells us that in Adam the whole human race sinned and fell.

**Worksheet 59**

From God's perspective, nothing happens by "chance" because He knows everything. However, chance can also mean "opportunity," which seems to be how you used it. In one sense, God did give Adam and Eve a second chance because He did not immediately eliminate them for their sin, which is what they deserved.

### Worksheet 60

God used the Israelites to judge the people and remove the evil in the land. We know there are still evil, wicked people today. But God doesn't command us to destroy those people in the same way. That is because Jesus Christ died on the cross. God judged the sin in the world by punishing His Son on the cross.

### Worksheet 61

God created us to glorify Him and to enjoy Him forever.

### Worksheet 62

In the Bible we are told that God has given His word to men to write down so we can know how everything came to be. The Bible, which is God's Word, though penned by man, tells us that God WAS there and He has given us an eyewitness account of exactly how the universe and everything in it was created.

### Worksheet 63

The Bible came from holy men of God. These men were inspired by God through the Holy Spirit working in their hearts.

### Worksheet 64

The Bible tells us that God spoke out loud to Moses many times as he led the Israelites to the Promised Land.

### Worksheet 65

We are able to confirm many aspects of the Bible's history in areas of science, such as geology and astronomy. We can also rely on the Bible's truth concerning Jesus — for instance, in considering how many prophecies about Him were made hundreds of years before He came to earth as a man. Because we can confirm the history in the Bible, we can have faith in all that the Bible has to say.

### Worksheet 66

It is a very sad situation here in America that in public schools there is much confusion about God and the Bible and what people can say or do. Many want to keep "religion" completely out of the schools. But when we try to keep God out of schools, we end up teaching the kids that there is no God.

### Worksheet 67

God is still a God of miracles today. We all pray for healing from sickness from time to time, either for ourselves or for others. God may or may not give physical healing at that time. God changing our hearts from desiring evil to desiring Him IS a wonderful miracle as well.

### Worksheet 68

People believe so many different things because they are sinners and they don't want to listen to God.

### Worksheet 69

1. Numbers 23:19
2. Revelation 1:8
3. Hebrews 1:1–2
4. 2 Peter 1:21
5. Romans 5:12
6. Jeremiah 23:24
7. 2 Peter 3:8
8. 2 Timothy 3:16
9. John 1:1–3
10. John 17:14

## Answers Book for Kids Volume 4 — Worksheet Answer Keys

### Worksheet 70

By creating Adam and Eve, God created beings to whom He could show His attributes — love, mercy, and so on.

### Worksheet 71

Our sin against God is so bad that it could only be paid for by Jesus Christ (the perfect One) suffering and dying in our place.

**Worksheet 72**

God promises His children, those who believe and trust in Jesus and live for Him, that He will never leave us.

**Worksheet 73**

When a soldier goes to war, it is not "murder" because he is obeying his orders and defending himself against the enemy. He is not doing it to be hateful, and he would stop fighting if the war was over.

**Worksheet 74**

Everyone will NOT be the same in heaven. We will be ourselves without sin.

**Worksheet 75**

In the end, God will judge all the "bad guys," even though, from our limited human perspective, it seems they often win.

**Worksheet 76**

Sin entered the world — to all of us — through Adam because we are his descendants. So, what about Satan? He was not the father of the human race (it was Adam) and he had not been given dominion over all the earth (that was Adam, too), so he is not the one responsible for sin in our world today. Adam's sin is considered the first sin.

**Worksheet 77**

The sin and vanity in Lucifer's heart came when he chose evil over good and stopped glorifying the One who created him.

**Worksheet 78**

They didn't do anything wrong. The Bible says that all things will die on earth because of Adam's sin in the Garden of Eden.

**Worksheet 79**

God made it clear that if Adam disobeyed Him by eating the fruit from the tree, then he would die. Because of that very first sin, all living things would have to die. Sickness is part of dying.

**Worksheet 80**

Tsunamis, death, divorce, earthquakes, floods, fighting . . . all the bad things in the world . . . are because of sin. It's not God's fault these things happen — it is because of sin.

**Worksheet 81**

Cain's heart was wicked and evil. He was angry and jealous of his brother and killed him out of envy.

**Worksheet 82**

People before Christ were saved by faith, and thus went to heaven when they died, and those who did not have faith were separated from God forever.

**Worksheet 83**

The Bible doesn't say for sure if Adam and Eve went to heaven or believed God's promise of the coming Savior, but the Bible shows that it is a good possibility.

**Worksheet 84**

The Bible refers to mansions in our Father's house. Will there really be mansions? It could be. But whatever Jesus is referring to here, we know that it will be something amazing that our minds can't even imagine. And the Bible tells us that one day we will have new physical bodies that will be different from the bodies we have now.

**Worksheet 85**

When we get to heaven, we will have perfect love for God, and He will be our primary and eternal desire. We will worship Him in full happiness and will never want to stop.

**Worksheet 86**

Being born again means becoming part of God's family — the word "again" literally means "from above" — becoming a child of God.

**Worksheet 87**

When God tells us that the mountains and the hills will cry out and the trees will clap their hands, God is describing joy and delight and praise that is really too great to even imagine.

**Worksheet 88**

Although Jesus only preached in the Middle East, His word is still spreading today as He commanded to happen. The Apostles — the word means "messengers" — took the gospel to the rest of the world because Jesus commanded them to take it to

Jerusalem, Judea, Samaria, and to the ends of the earth.

### Worksheet 89

Well, we don't know — but He was more sad than we could ever be.

### Worksheet 90

Remember God's wonderful plan of salvation that He had worked out before He created the universe! God wanted to show us how much He loved us by sending His only Son to earth, that whoever believes in Him will share eternal life with Him in heaven.

### Worksheet 91

First, any religion that claims to be true MUST believe that Jesus is God. Second, you must find out if they believe that salvation is given to those who trust in Jesus.

### Worksheet 92

1. 1 Corinthians 2:9
2. John 11:35
3. Matthew 28:19
4. Romans 11:33
5. Romans 8:22
6. 1 John 4:4
7. Mark 4:41
8. Acts 4:12
9. Romans 5:12
10. Hebrews 11:4

## Answers Book for Kids Volume 5 — Worksheet Answer Keys

### Worksheet 93

According to God's Word, bodies out in space, like the sun, moon, and stars, were created on day 4 of the creation week.

### Worksheet 94

To give light, for comparison, and to declare the glory of God.

### Worksheet 95

It is basically what is above the earth. This would include our atmosphere (inner space) and outer space. It's what you see when you stand outside and look up.

### Worksheet 96

A week comes from the Bible because God created in 6 days and He rested on the seventh day.

### Worksheet 97

Black holes are real objects that God made in space. Because they have so much mass, their gravity is so strong that light can't even escape from them. If light cannot escape a black hole, then it can never get to your eyes, so it appears black.

### Worksheet 98

The Bible seems to rule out any native intelligent life in outer space since they would be under the Curse with no possibility of salvation.

### Worksheet 99

The stripes that appear on the planet are actually generated by strong winds. Because of its gas composition and strong winds, it is prone to massive storms. The biggest storm on Jupiter is called the Great Red Spot, and it appears as a large red spot on the planet.

### Worksheet 100

Comets are icy objects in space that release dust or gas when they approach the sun. They are typically made of ice, dust, and frozen gases, and some even have a rocky core.

### Worksheet 101

The next closest galaxy is Canis Major Dwarf, which is about 25,000 light-years away.

### Worksheet 102

By this definition, there are only eight planets (Mercury, Venus, Earth, Mars, Jupiter, Saturn, Uranus, and Neptune). Although Pluto used to be considered the smallest planet, the smallest one is now Mercury. Mercury is also the closest planet to the sun. Planets have a fixed orbit at a certain distance around the sun, so none of them will ever collide. (UPDATE: By some definitions, Pluto is considered a lesser planet now.)

## Worksheet 103

An overwhelming number of Christians opposed a flat earth and for good reason. The Bible teaches against it in Isaiah 40:22 and Job 26:10. These verses point out that the earth is circular or round.

## Worksheet 104

Meteoroids, when they fall into earth's atmosphere, become "meteors." If some parts of a meteor don't burn up, those pieces are called "meteorites." Can they be dangerous? Yes, they can, but most are not. Most meteors typically burn up, with nothing left of them to fall out of the sky.

## Worksheet 105

The surface temperature of the sun is about 10,000° Fahrenheit (5778° Kelvin [K]). The coolest stars (under 3500°K) are red. Next on the scale are red-to-orange stars, with a temperature of 3500–5000°K. Then there are yellow-to-white stars, which range from 5000–6000°K. Next are stars in the white-to-blue range, with temperatures of 6000°K–7500°K. Blue stars are the hottest (typically over 7500°K).

## Worksheet 106

At this stage, we have sent something that has finally reached the outer edges of our solar system and is about to enter interstellar space. It is called the *Voyager 1* spacecraft and was launched in September of 1977.

## Worksheet 107

The rings are made up of dust, rock, and ice. Some of the particles are smaller than grains of sand but can be as large as a building.

## Worksheet 108

The supposed big bang is one of the popular atheistic models about the origin of the universe. It basically teaches that the universe created itself. There was nothing, then something popped into existence from nothing, rapidly "exploded," and is still expanding today.

## Worksheet 109

Our galaxy is called the Milky Way. It is about 12,000 light-years across (1 light year = almost 5.878625 trillion miles).

## Worksheet 110

As long as the earth endures, God promised that day and night, cold and heat, seedtime and harvest, and winter and summer shall not cease (Genesis 8:22).

## Worksheet 111

Comets are made mostly of dust, rock, and ice, while asteroids are primarily made of rock. A snowball hitting a rock might be similar to what it would be like if a comet hit an asteroid at high speed. So, the comet, depending on the size, would likely be the one that broke up more.

## Worksheet 112

God created the universe on day 1 and Adam on day 6. When we add up the genealogies in the Bible from Adam to Abraham in Genesis 5 and 11, it comes to about 2,000 years. Most people agree that Abraham lived about 2,000 B.C., which is approximately 4,000 years ago from today. So, we know the universe is around 6,000 years old.

## Worksheet 113

| O | E | S | A | R | Y | R | U | C | R | E | M | R | E |
|---|---|---|---|---|---|---|---|---|---|---|---|---|---|
| U | U | J | U | P | I | T | E | R | P | A | N | E | R |
| H | R | N | U | M | C | E | Y | X | A | L | A | G | E |
| M | E | A | I | T | E | A | S | T | E | R | O | I | D |
| S | K | N | N | V | R | T | E | N | U | T | P | E | N |
| M | A | S | U | U | E | R | E | H | A | U | M | E | A |
| O | M | T | H | R | S | R | U | O | P | A | E | M | O |
| O | E | R | U | S | S | V | S | N | R | U | V | T | A |
| N | K | E | U | R | V | E | M | E | T | S | U | H | E |
| S | A | N | S | R | N | N | C | U | E | L | P | T | S |
| R | M | I | R | A | R | U | A | O | P | T | K | R | K |
| S | R | M | R | T | L | S | E | E | M | S | R | A | M |
| E | L | H | N | S | R | A | T | S | T | E | K | E | O |
| S | E | L | O | H | K | C | A | L | B | I | T | E | R |

Elementary Apologetics 193

**Worksheet 114**

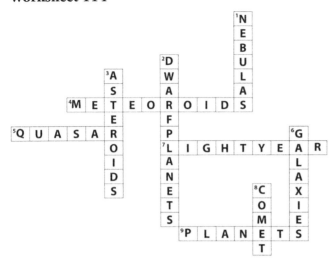

**Worksheet 115**

1. Ecclesiastes 7:17
2. Romans 1:20
3. Genesis 1:7
4. Job 38:31
5. Isaiah 55:9
6. Psalms 31:3
7. Genesis 1:1
8. Exodus 20:11
9. Colossians 1:16
10. Psalms 72:5

# Answers Book for Kids Volume 6 — Worksheet Answer Keys

## Worksheet 116

Noah's descendants found a plain between the Tigris and Euphrates rivers and dwelt there. That plain is where Babel was located. This small city of Babel and the region of Babylonia (the region was later named after the city of Babel) were in southern Mesopotamia, which is part of modern-day Iraq.

## Worksheet 117

Judging by the square base where the tower originally was located, an old description on a tablet, and the writing of a historian named Herodotus, the tower was probably about 7–8 stories and 300 feet (91 meters) high.

## Worksheet 118

A Jewish historian named Josephus, who lived about 2,000 years ago, said of the Tower of Babel, "It grew very high, sooner than anyone could expect," though the Bible doesn't tell us how long it actually took.

## Worksheet 119

The Bible in Genesis 10 gives a list of families that came out of Babel with new languages. Since we don't know how many people were in each family, we can't know the exact number of people who came out of Babel. If we add up the families, there were at least 78.

## Worksheet 120

The Tower of Babel incident occurred around 4,200 years ago — about 100 years after the Flood.

## Worksheet 121

The Tower of Babel is not around anymore. If it were, it would be over 4,200 years old.

## Worksheet 122

There really isn't much left of the Tower of Babel. Alexander the Great removed bricks and the outer coating, but he never rebuilt it. However, most researchers think they know where the foundation is located.

## Worksheet 123

As far as we know, there was nothing inside the tower. It makes more sense that it would have been solid bricks inside, just like a ziggurat tower you might build of stacked wooden blocks.

## Worksheet 124

God wanted them to fill the earth and take possession of it, but Noah's descendants decided to disobey God. Instead, they built a city and tower so that they would not be scattered across the earth.

## Worksheet 125

Yes. There was originally only one language, so if everyone had scattered over the earth, they would have continued to speak that language. It is possible that we would have various dialects as people lived in different parts of the world.

### Worksheet 126
There were a minimum of 78 language families and possibly a few more from Babel. If you tally the existing language families up around the world, there are less than 100 language families in the world today.

### Worksheet 127
We all have the same basic skin color, from the main pigment in our skin called "melanin." This pigment is a brown color. This means that humans are all brown in color, but they have different shades from dark to light.

### Worksheet 128
After the Flood, the Ice Age occurred. This caused the ocean levels to be lowered by as much as 350 feet. This would have opened up land bridges to places like North America, so that people could walk across.

### Worksheet 129
All people today came out of Babel (Genesis 10:32), including the Chinese people. The Chinese came from the line of Noah's son Ham and grandson Canaan.

### Worksheet 130
Many Americans, Australians, Canadians, and others are descendants of the English. Most of the English came from Germanic tribes of the northern part of mainland Europe, namely the Angles and Saxons. "Angles" is where we get the name English from (think "Anglish").

### Worksheet 131
A Spanish historian wrote that one of the earliest settlements on the island of Japan was by the family of Tarshish (one of Noah's great grandsons, who also inhabited one particular region of Spain), who was the son of Javan.

### Worksheet 132
The Ice Age was an event that happened after the Flood. At the end of the Flood, the oceans would have been warmer and the land cooler. This would have resulted in a lot of evaporation from the oceans and snow then falling on the land, resulting in a massive ice build-up on about one-third of the earth.

### Worksheet 133
For an ice age, we need warm oceans, cool land, and cool summers. With a warm ocean, this means more water would evaporate, resulting in more water in the air that would form more snow and ice, particularly in the wintertime.

### Worksheet 134
It covered most of Canada and parts of the upper United States as far down as Illinois, Indiana, and Ohio. In Europe, it extended over most of northern Europe, like Sweden, Norway, and Finland, and most of England. In Asia, it covered parts of northern Russia. The ice also affected southern areas like Antarctica and stretched across the ocean almost to the southern tip of South America.

### Worksheet 135
They have found a man frozen in a glacier. He is named "Ötzi, the Iceman." His body was found frozen in ice in the Alps Mountains between Italy and Austria.

### Worksheet 136
During the Ice Age, a lot of water was taken out of the oceans and accumulated on the land in the form of ice and snow. Most think that the ocean level dropped by about 350 feet! This drop would expose land bridges in different places throughout the world.

### Worksheet 137
These animals were primarily warm-blooded mammals. There were many animals that would do well, but the more famous ones were the saber-toothed cat, woolly mammoth, dire wolf, giant beaver, snowshoe hare (rabbit), mastodon, short-faced bear, musk ox, and many others, like types of shrews, moles, and skunks.

### Worksheet 138
1. Genesis 11:4
2. Luke 21:18
3. Proverbs 12:10
4. Job 38:29
5. Isaiah 49:12

6. Genesis 11:9
7. Job 6:16
8. Genesis 10:32
9. Genesis 11:8
10. Job 37:10

# Answers Book for Kids Volume 1–6 — Quiz Answer Keys

**Quiz 1**
1. power
2. pattern
3. different
4. 24
5. obey
6. proud
7. planets
8. Evolution
9. control
10. characteristics

**Quiz 2**
1. dinosaurs
2. sea
3. death
4. decayed
5. search
6. rose
7. petroglyphs
8. people
9. warm
10. melanin

**Quiz 3**
1. glory
2. infinite
3. sinned
4. judged
5. created
6. inspired
7. Moses
8. Jesus
9. schools
10. sinners

**Quiz 4**
1. F
2. T
3. T
4. F
5. T
6. F
7. F
8. T
9. T
10. T

**Quiz 5**
1. T
2. F
3. T
4. T
5. F
6. T
7. T
8. T
9. F
10. T

**Quiz 6**
1. 7–8
2. 78
3. 4,200
4. 100
5. melanin
6. English
7. Flood
8. Job
9. Ötzi
10. 350

## Daily Lesson Plans

### WE'VE DONE THE WORK FOR YOU

PERFORATED & 3-HOLE PUNCHED
FLEXIBLE 180-DAY SCHEDULE
DAILY LIST OF ACTIVITIES
RECORD KEEPING

"THE TEACHER GUIDE MAKES TH
SO MUCH EASIER AND TAKES
GUESS WORK OUT OF IT FOR

# HOMESCHOOL

Master Books® Homeschool Curricul

Faith-Building Books & Resources
Parent-Friendly Lesson Plans
Biblically-Based Worldview
Affordably Priced

Master Books® is the leading publisher of books and resources based upon a Biblical worldview that points to God as our Cre Now the books you love, from the authors you trust like Ken Ham, Michael Farris, Tommy Mitchell, and many more are available as a homeschool curriculum.

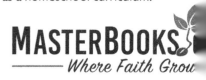